A PATH

Praise for...
A Path to Learning and Literacy

"This book is especially relevant during current times as educators, students, and parents navigate learning through online platforms. Machosky-Ullman's years of teaching expertise radiate throughout this book. The layout is easy to follow, and it is a must read for students struggling to organize at-home learning or daily homework assignments. **A Path to Learning and Literacy** is useful for any student whether they are just beginning a homework routine or attending college-level classes. In following Machosky-Ullman's suggestions in the book, all learners can greatly benefit from her succinct and practical tips!"

Jenny Mischel, PhD, Educational Psychology
Visiting Assistant Professor
Washington and Lee University
Lexington, Virginia
Mother of four children

"This highly practical book just made getting your kids on track even easier. Whether your kids just need a little extra push or are struggling, **A Path to Learning and Literacy** takes out the guess work for studying. All packed into one place, this easy step-by-step approach sets up the student for success. It pinpoints the real strategies and skills they need to build their academic potential. This book can be a life saver to parents and students alike."

Anna Maria Ventura, MBA, Marketing and Advertising
Educator and Parent of four children
Northern Virginia, Virginia

A PATH TO LEARNING AND LITERACY

"Formal schooling provides many opportunities to learn new material. However, learning habits occur at home. After reading this book you will immediately have the methods necessary to help your child develop life-long organizational and study strategies. In addition, these techniques are extremely beneficial for children with special needs and alternate learning styles."

Heather Cetina, M.Ed.
Private Consultant/Contractor
Elementary Education
Teacher of Visually Impaired
Long Island, New York
Parent of three children

"Through my observation, while teaching fluid mechanics at the university, so many undergraduates have the talent and ability but lack the proper studying skills to succeed in engineering courses. **A PATH TO LEARNING AND LITERACY** provides parents and students with the necessary directions to build a solid foundation of good study skills early in their academic career. These same study skills will be very beneficial and key to a successful and rewarding university education."

Lynn Albers
North Carolina State University
National Science Foundation
GK-12 Outreach Program Fellow
Mechanical and Aerospace Engineering Ph.D. Student, Thermal Sciences
Raleigh, North Carolina

A PATH TO LEARNING AND LITERACY

"The advice and strategies suggested in this work are sorely needed in the field of education. Although aimed at parents, this is a 'must read' for teachers as well. The work belongs on teachers' desks along with three other works of reference: dictionary, a thesaurus, and a grammar book. "

Audrey Capozzi
Adjunct Professor
Child Study Department
St. Joseph's College
Patchogue, New York

"Looking for ways to become a smart student? This is an excellent guide for parents and students alike. There are numerous useful techniques for any student to improve their study habits as well as their grades."

Gwen McHugh
Parent and Educator
Long Island, New York

"Finally, there is a tool for parents to guide their children to 'be on target' with all school assignments. This book shows your child how to assume responsibility and find the path to achieving goals. Parents will find it advantageous in reducing stress while attaining success."

Virginia Nolan
Author
Listening Tune-Ups for the Classroom
Riverhead, New York

A PATH TO LEARNING AND LITERACY

Mission Statement: To help you LEARN HOW TO STUDY. To assist students in their efforts to work toward improving their academic performance through a continuous process of routine study habits, an awareness of curriculum materials and requirements, and continuous self-assessment of individual performance and progress.

A Path to Learning and Literacy

Study Guide and Workbook
for Secondary Students and Parents
Second Edition

Claire Johnson Machosky

"Parents are the most important teachers
children will ever have."
—Claire Machosky

The contents of this work, including, but not limited to, the accuracy of events, people, and places depicted; opinions expressed; permission to use previously published materials included; and any advice given or actions advocated are solely the responsibility of the author, who assumes all liability for said work and indemnifies the publisher against any claims stemming from publication of the work.

Cover design by Catherine Machosky
Edited by Albert Ullman

All Rights Reserved
Copyright © 2020 by Claire Johnson Machosky

No part of this book may be reproduced or transmitted, downloaded, distributed, reverse engineered, or stored in or introduced into any information storage and retrieval system, in any form or by any means, including photocopying and recording, whether electronic or mechanical, now known or hereinafter invented without permission in writing from the publisher.

Dorrance Publishing Co
585 Alpha Drive
Suite 103
Pittsburgh, PA 15238
Visit our website at *www.dorrancebookstore.com*

ISBN: 978-1-6491-3427-1
eISBN: 978-1-6491-3559-9

A PATH TO LEARNING AND LITERACY

Copyright © Machosky, Claire Johnson A PATH TO LEARING AND LITERACY Study Directions for Students and Parents 2009. All rights reserved. Second Edition – 2020.

      Credits:

           Editor: Anne Gardner
           Cover design: Catherine Machosky
           Publisher:
           Printer:

No part of this book may be reproduced in whole or part, or stored in a retrieval system or transmitted in any form by electronic means, electronic, mechanical, photocopying, recording or otherwise, without permission of the author and the publisher.

A PATH TO LEARNING AND LITERACY

This book is dedicated to my students.

They taught me the intricacies of successful learning.

Through the pages in this book, I hope to share these insights and strategies with today's students and parents.

Special thanks to my husband, Al Ullman, for his encouragement and assistance.

A PATH TO LEARNING AND LITERACY

INTRODUCTION

My intention in writing this book is to share with students and parents a variety of learning routines and study strategies that produce results.

Throughout the book whenever I use the term YOU, I am referring to the student and what he/she should be doing. Each chapter focuses on answering the **Chapter Question** with specific suggestions for improving learning and literacy. Students have two other segments in each chapter for easy reference – **Frequently Asked Questions** and **Chapter Check Up.** **Frequently Asked Questions** provides key information regarding the chapter in question form. The **Chapter Check Up** is a handy review for you to apply the key elements of each chapter.

The final segment in each chapter is entitled, **A Note to Parents;** it gives specific recommendations and information to parents, guardians, and other adults regarding the theme of the chapter.

The step-by-step process I describe provides essential building blocks in the learning process. It is important to follow these steps to establish routines that increase learning and literacy. The book has three distinct sections. The first section is entitled **GETTING STARTED** – it guides you through the steps of deciding where and when you will do work at home as well as techniques for understanding, following, and completing your lessons and assignments. Section two, **PROGRESS,** emphasizes various study strategies. Section three,

A PATH TO LEARNING AND LITERACY

ACCOMPLISHMENT, explains how to reflect on your individual progress. Section four of the book contains suggested **STUDY GUIDES** that can be adapted for use with different subjects.

The four content sections of the book are followed by **The Workbook for A Path to Learning and Literacy**. There is an activity worksheet for each chapter that assists you to identify and build your understanding of how to learn and study. **The Workbook** also includes Self-Assessment and Achievement worksheets that are designed to individualize your learning, establish your routines, and monitor your progress.

When you, the student, understand what you are supposed to do and align your study habits to accommodate your abilities, you will reduce the frustration and stress that can come from doing schoolwork. All study time is time spent on *A Path to Learning and Literacy.* It is my intent that with the use of this book your personal education path will be productive, satisfying, rewarding, and successful.

A PATH TO LEARNING AND LITERACY

A Note to Parents:

Parents are the most important teachers their children will ever have. Children will always look to their parents for guidance and support. Children value all adults who contribute to their development, although they rarely admit it.

The procedures outlined in this book will help parents, guardians and other concerned adults become positive role models in valuing education for children. Young children will need adult coaching to help them understand the content of the book. Secondary students will be able to read and use the book on their own; but they always value parental input. Parents, guardians, and tutors will find individualized chapter coaching tips that explain how the role of the guide on the side is most effective.

Remember we are in the INFORMATION AGE. For education, this means the INTERNET and INSTRUCTIONAL TECHNOLOGY are integral parts of learning. Online instruction is commonplace and communicating with the school is done virtually. Your children will do research and prepare assignments using the computer. They will also use the internet for recreational activities. Help your children distinguish between playing online and using the computer as a learning tool. It is important for parents and students to become familiar with the online resources that your school offers. It will vary, but most schools offer assignments online, parent/teacher communication portals, and online instruction.

A PATH TO LEARNING AND LITERACY

Table of Contents

SECTION 1 – GETTING STARTED   p.13

Chapter 1   Location, Time, and Materials:
Where, when and with what will you work and study?   p.14

Chapter 2   Identifying the Task:
What does the assignment require you to do?
                                                                    p.26

Chapter 3   Process:
What is your plan to accomplish the task?   p.36

SECTION 2 – PROGRESS   p.47

Chapter 4   Listening:
What information is being communicated?   p.48

Chapter 5   Learning:
How do you acquire new information?   p.58

Chapter 6   Studying:
Do you know how to study?   p.70

A PATH TO LEARNING AND LITERACY

Table of Contents

SECTION 3 – ACCOMPLISHMENT   p.83

Chapter 7   Evaluation:
How is your academic performance?   *p.84*

Chapter 8   Achievement:
What have you accomplished?   *p.94*

Chapter 9   Celebration:
Are you ready to celebrate?   *p.106*

SECTION 4 – STUDY GUIDES   p.117

Introduction to Study Guides	*p.118*
Key Words	*p.120*
Vocabulary Lists	*p.122*
Study Charts	*p.125*
Visual Webs	*p.127*
Summaries	*p.130*
Verbalizations	*p.132*

THE WORKBOOK   p. 135

ABOUT THE AUTHOR   p.185

A PATH TO LEARNING AND LITERACY

SECTION 1 – GETTING STARTED

Chapter 1 - Location, Time, and Materials
Chapter 2 - Identifying the Task
Chapter 3 - Process

A PATH TO LEARNING AND LITERACY

Chapter 1
Location, Time, and Materials

A PATH TO LEARNING AND LITERACY

Chapter 1   Location, Time, and Materials:

Where, when and with what will you work and study?

> Routines are essential to learning.
> Materials make learning efficient.

It is essential for you to establish a routine for learning. Think about where you would like to study, what time works best for you, and what you will need. You must realize that doing schoolwork at home is part of your daily routine – just like brushing your teeth or practicing for a sport or learning to play a musical instrument. Deciding on a location where you will work is the first major decision to be made in creating your routine. Give careful thought to your choice of location. You will need a place where you can create an atmosphere for studying. Where will you be comfortable and the most productive? You will want a location that is relatively quiet and conducive to concentrating on your work.

Many students enjoy working at the kitchen table or the dining room table because they have enough room to spread out and still feel connected to the family. Others prefer to work at a desk in their rooms. If you can honestly tell yourself there are no other distractions in your room that could be a good place to work. If there is a family room or den with a designated desk or workspace that could be a suitable location as well. Whichever place you choose, it must be

A PATH TO LEARNING AND LITERACY

available on a daily basis. You will want a surface where you can sit and work without being disturbed. Give careful thought to your choice of location. I repeat, you must create an atmosphere for studying. You should discuss your choice of location with your parents and let them know you will need the space daily for studying. If you have any specific requests for workspace you should discuss them with your parents.

NOTE: When you work with other students use these same strategies for deciding where to work. If working together online, planning is essential. You will need a location that will be comfortable and productive with a minimum of interference.

Consider your overall schedule when deciding on a time for schoolwork. You should feel rested and not under stress. If you have after school activities be sure to take a break and build in a relaxation period before starting your assignments. Examples of a relaxation period include watching a select TV show, talking on the phone with friends, or playing outside. Another consideration before you begin your assignments is – do you need a snack before or some finger food while working? This will help you concentrate and prevent distractions.

When will online instruction or doing assignments take place? Establishing a routine time to work is essential. Again, take charge of making this decision. Be sure to consider established times for online lessons and then the time of day that will be most productive for your homework time. It should be the same each day. Also, the amount of time

A PATH TO LEARNING AND LITERACY

scheduled should be routine, although it could vary slightly depending on the amount of homework. In addition to doing your daily assignments, homework time should be used to review the work you did in school that day and organize your notes, papers, and other materials.

How much time you will spend on homework will vary according what needs to be done. Routines are essential to developing good study habits. Therefore, you should set aside a specific amount of time each day for schoolwork. Routinely it should be at least a half hour and could be as long as two hours. This will allow adequate time to create your personal atmosphere for learning. It will take a few minutes to focus your attention on your studying. A good way to begin your study session is to review your day at school. Get ready to do homework by identifying your task (see chapter two) to determine what you need to read, what you need to research and what written work is required. After completing your homework take the time to summarize and check how you spent your homework session.

Once you have identified the location and time for doing homework you must consider the tools you will need. It is important to have all the necessary materials for homework readily available. Your list of supplies includes agenda books or assignment pads, notebooks, pens, pencils, paper, a dictionary, a calculator, computer, cell phone, etc. Supply needs will be very individual, so it is important for you to make a personal list and assemble all your supplies. If you are working at a table, you will need to get a storage box to store your supplies. You can open the box and immediately have

A PATH TO LEARNING AND LITERACY

what is needed for a productive homework session. See the Material Check list in the CHAPTER CHECK UP section at the end of this chapter for suggestions to make your own Materials' Checklist. If you are using a computer or phone, be sure to stay focused on your homework needs during your study session.

Do not forget your most important tool, the ASSIGNMENT PAD or AGENDA BOOK. The assignment pad/agenda book is the student's daily planner. In the assignment pad you should put the date and record your assignments in detail. This will help you understand what you are required to do. It will help you plan and organize your study time and provide the specifics of an assignment when you have questions. It is important to do this for online classes.

Finally, make your home study location a quiet cell phone free zone. Your homework session should not be interrupted by phone calls, text messages or emails. The use of technology for personal use will interfere with your ability to concentrate and your productivity. Your cell phone should be used only as a learning tool while you are doing schoolwork.

A PATH TO LEARNING AND LITERACY

Frequently Asked Questions

➢ **How do I learn to make decisions?** *You learn to make decisions by assuming responsibilities. You can participate in decision making with your parents and show how you can handle more and more responsibility.*

➢ **What is the best location for doing schoolwork?** *A workable location will be different for different people. The most important criteria is selecting a location that enables you to focus on the task at hand.*

➢ **When should I do homework?** *You should establish a routine time to do homework every day. This time should be used to review notes and class work and to complete all your reading and written assignments.*

➢ **How much time should I spend doing homework?** *This will depend on the length and demands of your assignment(s). It will also vary according to your own pacing. Time spent on doing homework is very individual.*

➢ **What do I need to work efficiently?** *You need to have all your supplies and materials in one location when you begin working.*

A PATH TO LEARNING AND LITERACY

- ➢ ***Why do I need an assignment pad or agenda book?*** *It is easier to keep track of your required assignments and when they are due when you write them down. The assignment pad is a student's daily planner. It will help you develop strong organizational skills.*

- ➢ ***How do I get ready to work effectively?*** *Know where and when you'll work and identify what materials and supplies you will need to do your homework. Have your supplies readily available. Check your assignment pad and determine which texts and other resources you will need before getting to work.*

- ➢ ***What is the effect of doing daily homework and review?*** *Research has proven that daily review of schoolwork greatly increases retention and understanding of content. Doing daily homework reinforces the content knowledge.*

A PATH TO LEARNING AND LITERACY

CHAPTER CHECK UP

Check Your Understanding

Answer the following questions:
- Is my work area comfortable?
- Where will I be doing my homework?
- When will I be doing my homework?
- Am I working alone or with others?
- What supplies do I need?
- Did I remember an assignment pad?

Check Your Progress

Apply these strategies.
- Establish daily routines for studying.
- Locate the place and time you will be studying.
- Organize your supplies.
- Review your schoolwork and your homework assignments.
- Begin homework on schedule and without distractions.
- Be prepared for the next level of work.

A PATH TO LEARNING AND LITERACY

Checklist

Advance your progress by assembling all your supplies.
- Pens & pencils
- Paper
- Assignment Pad
- Notebooks
- Textbooks
- Reference sources – i.e. dictionary, charts, formulas, computer, computer programs, disks, websites, homework assignments, hot line phone numbers and/or websites.

A PATH TO LEARNING AND LITERACY

A Note to Parents

When parents are working with their children, they should discuss with them where and when they would like to work. It is important that children feel ownership in making the decisions about doing schoolwork.

Parents and children must discuss the responsibility of the decisions and the importance of finding the right place and time to work to get the job done.

- ➢ Young children especially need the closeness to adults and will work best at a desk in the family room or at the kitchen table.

- ➢ Older children often feel the need for independence and may prefer working separately in their rooms or in a family den or office.

- ➢ There may be times when it is beneficial for children to work together on a project. This will require a third type of location. It could involve scheduling online conference time.

A PATH TO LEARNING AND LITERACY

> ➤ *Depending on the task, parents should listen to their children and discuss what will work best. Then parents and children can jointly decide on a workable location.*

When determining a time schedule for daily assignments with your children ask them when they would be most productive working. Consider your children's schedules beyond school when deciding time for schoolwork.

> ➤ *For pre-school and primary school children the amount of time needed will range from 10 minutes to perhaps 30-40 minutes.*

> ➤ *For upper elementary school children, the amount of time will range from a half hour to perhaps an hour or a little more.*

> ➤ *For middle school children the amount of time will range from 40 minutes to perhaps an hour and a half.*

> ➤ *For high school students the amount of time will range from one to two hours or more depending on assignments and other circumstances.*

Successful planning involves assembling the necessary materials needed for doing homework. For example, a child

A PATH TO LEARNING AND LITERACY

can be easily distracted when he/she cannot find a pencil. Create and/or review a Materials Checklist when setting up the location and time for doing homework. Include an assignment pad or agenda book in the school study materials and take the time to explain to your child the importance of recording assignment daily. It is the tool that tells a student what to do! Have a Materials Box available for your child to place homework resources in. You are the role model for your child. Helping him/her to establish the routine of where, when, and how to do homework will be greatly appreciated.

Remember each person learns differently and works at his/her own pace. The above are guidelines and an individual's performance will vary. The key is to not let the amount of time spent on homework become a source of stress.

The role of parents is so very important at every age. Children work to please their parents. Therefore, parents must continuously demonstrate their interest in their child's performance. Help your child get started, be a supporter and check for the completion of the assignments. Most importantly - Give praise for a job well done! Always find something positive to say about the time spent on schoolwork and homework. Your children need your approval and the more they receive it, the better it is for them. Children never outgrow the need to please their parents.

A PATH TO LEARNING AND LITERACY

Chapter 2
Identifying the Task

A PATH TO LEARNING AND LITERACY

Chapter 2   Identifying the Task:

What does the assignment require you to do?

> *Verbalize the task.*
> *Know the assignment specifics.*

Once you have established your Location, Time, and Supply List for doing schoolwork, it is important to **Identify the Task**. You must know what you are expected to do. The best way to demonstrate your understanding of the task is to verbalize it. You do this by putting the assignment or task in your own words. Even better, explain the task to your parents or another student. This process clarifies the task and will make you aware of any questions that still need to be answered.

NOTE: When you are working in a group, you need to discuss the task with everyone in the group. The group should discuss the task, raise, discuss, answer questions, and agree on what is to be done. Once the task is clearly identified, a plan for completing the assignment can be easily constructed. (See Process, Chapter 3)

If you find there are questions that you cannot answer while identifying the task you need to find those answers before completing your work. To find answers, you should review the given assignment for details. You should make notes on the requirements you must meet and the steps

A PATH TO LEARNING AND LITERACY

you must take in doing the assignment. If you still have questions, ask your teacher to explain the assignment again. If you are working with your teacher online, be sure to write out the questions you want to ask. Listen carefully to your teacher's explanation and then tell him/her what you heard. This act of repeating the assignment in your own words will confirm your understanding of the task. If necessary, you could even take notes while talking with your teacher. Do not worry, your teacher will welcome the opportunity to clarify the task. Teachers want you to succeed. This dialogue with your teacher is important and builds your communication skills and reinforces your understanding of what you are doing.

Details are key elements in producing quality assignments. You should be able to identify the different parts of the assignment. For example, a typical reading and writing assignment requires many steps. When you are beginning the assignment identify the textbook pages you should be using as a reference. These pages supply the basic information you will need to understand a topic. Do you have class notes that supplement the textbook information? Will using that information help you in completing your task? Finally, what are the written requirements? Do you have to answer questions, draw diagrams, give examples, summarize? These elements are all part of knowing the task.

Pay attention to the date when the assignment is expected to be completed. The amount of time you are given to do an assignment is directly related to what is expected. The due date is very important! If you are doing a daily assignment it will be connected to your class work. The task will be focused and specific. If you are working on a project that will be due in two weeks, it will involve more research and comprehensive writing. You will have to schedule your time over the two weeks to complete all parts of the project. Always make sure to complete all your assignments on time. This shows effort and responsibility.

When you finish an assignment take the time to review what you learned by completing the assignment. This is a strategy to keep you focused, and it builds your long-term memory and knowledge of the subject.

Once you are clear on what you are doing, you will have a positive feeling about doing the assignment and a good feeling about the subject. You will have used your time constructively to produce quality work and gain knowledge. You feel good! This is the intrinsic reward for a job well done!

A PATH TO LEARNING AND LITERACY

Frequently Asked Questions

- **Why should I verbalize an assignment?** *If you can successfully verbalize your assignment it means you understand what you are expected to do and learn.*

- **What is meant by the assignment specifics?** *This refers to what you should produce to demonstrate learning or prepare for a level of understanding that will be reinforced in class. It could include reading, answering questions, writing, or some form of demonstrating.*

- **What if I do not understand what I'm to do and have questions?** *If you do not understand something you are expected to do, you must ask your teacher to explain it again. Remember, the only silly question is the one not asked.*

- **When is the assignment due?** *Most homework is assigned daily, but some research or long-term assignments may be spread over a longer period. This is especially true for the upper elementary grades and the secondary school. Know the due date and submit your work on time*

A PATH TO LEARNING AND LITERACY

➢ **What resources should I use to complete the assignment?** Resources are the materials that contain information you will need to complete the assignment. Resources could include the textbook, worksheets, websites, or other materials.

➢ **What are manipulatives and how do I use them?** Manipulatives are hands-on materials such as different colored chips or dice that help you to visually understand a concept. They are frequently used in explaining mathematics.

➢ **How should I prepare my assignment or project?** You should follow the guidelines your teacher gives you to complete the assignment. Assignments can be done on the computer and submitted online or written on loose-leaf paper, a worksheet, or in a notebook. Follow the teacher's direction!

➢ **What have I learned?** You should be able to explain in your own words the important facts, ideas, and activities that were taught during class time and/or acquired by completing your homework. This is another opportunity to practice the skill of verbalizing! (See Section 4 – Study Guides)

A PATH TO LEARNING AND LITERACY

CHAPTER CHECK UP

Check Your Understanding

Answer the following questions:
- Do I know what to do in completing an assignment?
- Do I have questions?
- When is the assignment due?
- What resources do I need to use?
- How is the assignment to be prepared?
- What have I learned?

Check Your Progress

Apply these strategies.
- Verbalize what is to be done.
- Give the specifics of how to do it.
- Locate the sources of information that will be used to help you complete the task.
- Complete the assignment using accurate information.
- Answer all parts of the assignment.
- Check your assignment before submitting.

A PATH TO LEARNING AND LITERACY

Checklist

Advance your progress. Use this checklist to determine if your assignment is complete.

- ➢ My assignment answers all questions and parts of questions.
- ➢ I have shown all required work.
- ➢ I have followed the required format.
- ➢ My work is neat and legible.
- ➢ The assignment is on time.
- ➢ I know the new information I have learned by doing the assignment.

A PATH TO LEARNING AND LITERACY

A Note to Parents:

Doing homework is a building block exercise. It is important to establish a strong foundation to develop effective study habits. Therefore, it is important to have your children develop successful routines from their first experiences in school. Habits and routines developed early will stay with your children throughout their school years and beyond. When children know what to do in completing homework their stress level is reduced. Therefore, verbalizing their assignment as part of Identifying the Task is extremely helpful.

A key consideration in **Identifying the Task** is your child's grade level in school.

- ➢ For pre-school and primary school children, tasks will usually include worksheets, hands-on manipulatives, (see Chapter 2 FAQs) and short reading and writing exercises.

- ➢ For upper elementary school children, tasks will be more complex and involve many different subjects. They will also involve worksheets, hands-on manipulatives, note taking, reading, writing, listening and some research.

- ➢ For middle school children, tasks will be varied depending on the subject being studied and the individual requirements of the teacher. There may be some worksheets and manipulatives, but there will be a

A PATH TO LEARNING AND LITERACY

growing emphasis on students completing short- and long-term assignments that require a variety of reading, writing, listening, researching and technology skills.

> For high school students, tasks will reflect the rigorous demands of the high school curriculum. Students will be expected to refine previous skills in completing routine homework as well as long term comprehensive written and performance activities and assignments.

Remember children learn best when they know what they are supposed to be learning. **Identifying the Task** and establishing a successful routine for reinforcing learning through homework assignments and projects are essential skills that develop success in school. The key is for parents to continually communicate with their children about their schoolwork. Parents may want to note the due date of major assignments on a big calendar and remind their child of the upcoming assignment and its due date.

A PATH TO LEARNING AND LITERACY

Chapter 3
Process

A PATH TO LEARNING AND LITERACY

Chapter 3 Process:

What is your plan to accomplish the task?

> **Start with the end in mind.**
> **Work smart.**

Process is your plan for completing your homework. In the two previous chapters you have learned how to design your routines for studying and you've practiced how to specifically state what your assignment requires. Now it is time to get the work done effectively and efficiently.

Begin by imagining the excellent assignment grade; now think about what needs to be done to achieve that goal. Imagine how to achieve the best score possible on an individual research paper or group project and think about the steps needed to get there. This is called **starting with the end in mind.** You identify your goal and then work backwards to design the use of time and resources to achieve that goal. For everyday homework it means visualizing what needs to be done and then using your time efficiently to do the work. For larger projects it means scheduling your time over a week or a month. This is a time management skill and it is an essential learning strategy. For long term projects you could use a calendar to plan when you would need to do the different parts of the project to help you organize each phase - research, planning and presentation.

A PATH TO LEARNING AND LITERACY

Working smart means you use your time efficiently. You work at a pace that you are comfortable with to understand the material and to get the job done. Although you may not finish your work fast, you will get more done and achieve higher quality work when you use effective time management strategies. To develop time management strategies, you need to determine the amount of time needed to complete a task or assignment and then add 10% more time. This will automatically build into your work schedule time for any additional research, time to rewrite materials, and time to summarize and review. These are all qualities that reinforce learning.

The challenge is to define how you will do the work. Chances are the teacher has given you an explanation and/or a sample of the work you are expected to do. You must pay attention to this. It is a model for you to follow. Copy the assignment into your Assignment Pad/Agenda Book and review it to see if you have any questions. If you do, ask them!

Does the assignment include reading? If it does, remember, reading is essential to learning. Don't fall into the habit of skipping the reading and just skimming for answers. Skipping the assigned reading is more time consuming than doing the reading and answering the questions. Reading is an excellent use of the 10% time factor you built into doing homework.

To improve your reading skills, practice the time-honored method of previewing. **Previewing** acquaints you with the material before reading it and therefore, speeds up

A PATH TO LEARNING AND LITERACY

your reading and your comprehension. These are the steps to follow in previewing. **SQ3R**

> ➤ **Scan** or look over the material to be read. Note: all bold face type, italics, etc. This procedure will acquaint you with the highlights of the reading.

> ➤ **Question** by turning bold faced headings into **questions.** As you read formulate the answer to the questions. For example, if the bold-faced print says LEADERSHIP QUALITIES, you will read to answer the question, WHAT ARE LEADERSHIP QUALITIES? By doing this you are building your comprehension skills.

> ➤ **3R Read** the content, **Recite** aloud the key points you have read, and **Review** the material by looking back over the pages. Now you are ready to answer questions. By continuously applying this process, you will increase your speed of reading, your comprehension, and your ability to answer questions with insight and example.

When doing written homework, you should be aware of how it will be evaluated because this will give you insights into how to prepare the assignment. For example:

A PATH TO LEARNING AND LITERACY

- ➤ Is there a required heading for the homework paper?

- ➤ If the work is being done on loose-leaf paper, do the assignment page numbers, etc. need to be written on the paper?

- ➤ Do answers have to be written in complete sentences?

- ➤ Do you need to include examples?

- ➤ Will the assignment be graded? If so, how?

- ➤ Is there a computer template to follow? Online date to submit assignment?

Process is ongoing; it is daily learning. Once you have established your learning routines it will be easier to sit down to attend online classes, to do your homework and find success. Reading textbooks and other assignments carefully for key information gives meaning to your written assignments; you will see your assignments as part of the total learning picture. Additionally, you will see connections between instruction, homework, and class work. Step-by-step you will begin to realize you are acquiring the discipline that learning requires.

A PATH TO LEARNING AND LITERACY

Frequently Asked Questions

- **What is starting with the end in mind?** When you imagine the very best in your schoolwork, you set a quality goal and can visualize the steps you'll need to follow in order to attain that goal.

- **What is meant by working smart?** This means to work efficiently at your own pace. The result will be that you will learn the information more thoroughly and the quality of your work will be better.

- **Is time management important?** Yes! When you have a realistic idea of how much time you will spend on a task you reduce your frustration level as well as stress. Always add 10% more time to your work schedule to increase your ability to work smart.

- **Why preview reading assignments?** When you preview reading assignments it makes them easier to read and understand. Previewing is a system for highlighting key ideas in the content to be read. The more you apply it, the stronger and easier your reading will become. You will build your reading comprehension and increase your speed.

A PATH TO LEARNING AND LITERACY

- ➤ **How do I use organizational skills in doing homework?** You plan exactly what needs to be done. You need to know what you are expected to do to complete the assignment. Make and use a checklist to avoid careless omissions.

- ➤ **Why do I need to know how my assignments will be graded?** When you know and understand the system your teacher uses to evaluate your work, you will have insights into how to produce the work that will satisfy the teacher's demands.

A PATH TO LEARNING AND LITERACY

CHAPTER CHECK UP

Check Your Understanding

Answer the following questions:
- What is the assignment and when is it due?
- What are my expectations for completing the assignment? **Remember to start with the end in mind.**
- What is my plan for studying – reading, writing? **Study Smart**
- Do I have everything I need to study?
- How much time do I think I need? **Remember to add 10% additional time.**
- Am I becoming disciplined in doing my homework?

Check Your Progress

Apply these strategies.
- Keep an Assignment Pad/ Agenda Book that is accurate and helpful.
- Plan how to use your time before you begin your homework.
- Preview Reading Assignments and read for information and understanding.
- Learn how assignments will be scored/graded and use that information in preparing assignments.
- Discipline yourself to follow your daily routine for studying and completing assignments.

A PATH TO LEARNING AND LITERACY

Checklist

Advance your progress. Use this checklist to determine that your assignment is complete.

- ➢ My homework headings and formats follow teacher's guidelines.
- ➢ I did the required reading.
- ➢ I answered all questions and parts of questions.
- ➢ I reviewed my work for accuracy.
- ➢ I asked my parents to check for any errors.
- ➢ I am confident because my work is complete, and my assignment will be on time.

A PATH TO LEARNING AND LITERACY

A Note to Parents

Children must do their own homework, but the parent can be the guide on the side. Younger children find encouragement when a parent sits with them while they work or is nearby to offer continued encouragement.

As children get older, they may want to work more independently, but they never outgrow the need for a parent's confirmation of their abilities. Therefore, parents should review homework assignments and offer constructive comments and most importantly, compliments. Don't forget to follow up by asking your child to give you feedback and report the results of his/her work. What grade did he/she receive? What comments did the teacher make? How does your child feel about the results?

This continuous communication between parent and child will reinforce positive work habits. The following suggestions are ways to encourage discussing schoolwork with your children.

- Ask your children about their goals and listen to what they want to do. Discuss how they could achieve their goals. Their input will give you insights on how to help them **Start with the End in Mind.**

- Encourage young children to discuss what their teacher has demonstrated in the classroom. Also, parents should check folders and book bags for teacher handouts.

A PATH TO LEARNING AND LITERACY

- ➢ Encourage older children to discuss how and why they are doing an assignment and any feedback they have received from previous work.

- ➢ Routinely check your child's Assignment Pad/Agenda Book. Be sure he/she is keeping current with assignments and that the assignments are detailed.

- ➢ When calculating the amount of time an assignment will take, add about 10% more time. This will help your child develop the skill of **working smart**.

- ➢ Help your children with planning long-range assignments and with determining how to use their time efficiently. Try plotting the study schedule on a calendar.

- ➢ Read to and with your children. If you are reading a textbook, ask them to explain what they have read. Use the preview strategies to build comprehension and speed.

- ➢ Examine your child's schoolwork and ask what he/she has accomplished in doing a specific homework. Does your child feel he/she understands the topic?

A PATH TO LEARNING AND LITERACY

SECTION 2 PROGRESS

Chapter 4 – Listening
Chapter 5 – Learning
Chapter 6 – Studying

A PATH TO LEARNING AND LITERACY

Chapter 4
LISTENING

A PATH TO LEARNING AND LITERACY

Chapter 4   Listening:

What information is being communicated?

> Active listening increases positive performance.
> Feedback requires listening.

Listening and Feedback are key learning skills that are frequently overlooked. You already know how to listen in your everyday situations or on the phone. Now you need to apply that same level of concentration to listening in the classroom and to online lessons. When your friends comment on what you are wearing, that is feedback. You value your friends' opinions and you react to their suggestions. The same is true with your teacher's comments about schoolwork. You should want to listen to your teacher's comments because they are giving you the feedback or suggestions on how to improve your work.

You should be listening in the classroom to the content of lessons. You need to listen to instructions when they are given. To maximize these listening skills, you will want to learn to become an active listener. This means you will be able to convey what you've heard with a high level of accuracy and retention. To become an active listener, you need to focus your attention on the person speaking, hear what they are saying, and observe their gestures. If you have correctly done active listening, you can repeat the information you have heard back to the speaker or to another class member. Is the

A PATH TO LEARNING AND LITERACY

message you repeated the same as the message the speaker conveyed? If it is, congratulations! If it is not, you need to develop your listening skills. You can do this easily by playing the old-fashioned game of telephone. Start by whispering a phrase to one person who passes it on to another person and continue the process to everyone in the room. What is the final phrase recited by the last person to hear it? How would you rate the listening skills that were used? Realize that listening is a learned skill that improves with practice. Good listening skills will also give you a deeper understanding of topics being discussed.

Another form of listening is receiving feedback. When you complete an assignment and ask your parents to check it, they may have a question or a comment. Don't become defensive at their inquiry but listen to their feedback. Use the active listening strategy mentioned above to repeat their message making sure you understand what they are saying. Once you understand their message, you can explain your answer and do some self-evaluating. Based on the conversation you may want to adjust your assignment. Remember, active listening increases performance quality.

Teacher feedback can be oral or in the form of grades and comments. You need to listen carefully to all teacher feedback. Each of the comments made by your teacher should be repeated in your own words to test the accuracy of what you are hearing. Now use your active listening skills to turn receiving feedback into a positive learning situation. Are the comments positive or negative? Did you receive suggestions for improvement? What steps should you take because of the feedback? Paying attention to all feedback is a form of listening. Remember, listening and receiving feedback are learning skills that can produce positive results and are keys to building success.

A teacher's written comments on your work are valuable tools to help you improve. Be sure to read them and react to them positively. For example, a comment such as **more details** could refer to the need to include examples to support your answer. This is the teacher's way of telling you that you could improve your performance by illustrating your facts or giving examples. You may want to discuss the comment with your teacher and ask for his/her recommendations for improvement. Remember, do not become defensive! LISTEN! Your teacher will welcome the opportunity to answer your questions, to discuss your work and offer suggestions on how to improve it. By listening attentively to your teacher's feedback, you will gain insights into your personal study habits and gain increased knowledge of the subject matter.

Listening and giving feedback are everyday skills that play a unique role in learning and studying. Become aware of them; apply them in the classroom; use them in preparing and reviewing schoolwork. You will be amazed at the results.

A PATH TO LEARNING AND LITERACY

Frequently Asked Questions

- ***What is the role of listening and feedback in learning?*** *These everyday skills when applied to the classroom make you more involved in learning. Listening gives you the information you need to do your work and feedback lets you know how you are doing.*

- ***What is Active Listening?*** *It is listening to understand what the other person is saying. If you listen actively you can tell the person what he/she has been saying.*

- ***When do I use Active Listening?*** *Active Listening is an ongoing process in learning. It should be used in all classes and with all assignments.*

- ***What is the Telephone Game?*** *It is a communication game where the person beginning the game whispers a phrase to a second person. The whispers continue from person to person until everyone in the room has participated. The last person repeats the phrase aloud. Almost always the message has changed and sometimes it changes drastically.*

A PATH TO LEARNING AND LITERACY

- **Why is feedback important?** We all need feedback to help us understand how we are doing. It is a way to determine if we are meeting expectations and if not, what needs to be done so we can meet those expectations.

- **Why do teachers give feedback?** Teachers want you to succeed. Their comments and suggestions are means of evaluating your work and showing you how to make improvements.

- **How do I use feedback?** You use feedback to improve your performance. Carefully review oral comments and written suggestions to identify what specific steps will help you to improve, then make a conscience effort to use those steps to improve your work.

A PATH TO LEARNING AND LITERACY

CHAPTER CHECK UP

Check Your Understanding

Answer the following questions:
- Are you listening for understanding during class?
- Do you write down your assignments using complete details?
- Do you understand and follow instructions?
- Do you ask others to review your work?
- Do you listen to others for suggestions?
- Do you revise your work when suggestions are offered?

Check Your Progress

Apply these strategies.
- Actively listen to others.
- Discuss what you hear for better understanding.
- Follow directions.
- Appreciate feedback.
- Apply suggestions to improve your work.

Checklist

Advance your progress. Use this checklist to improve your work.
- I review feedback on homework & class work.
- I react positively to feedback because it shows me how to improve.
- I listen for understanding in class.
- I ask questions when I don't understand something.
- I make changes that will bring positive improvements.
- I discuss with my teacher any suggestions that I don't completely understand.

A PATH TO LEARNING AND LITERACY

Note to Parents

Listening is so important to everyone at every stage of life. Parents must listen to their children. When you do your children become more willing to talk with you and share their thoughts and feelings. They feel valued.

Children always appreciate positive feedback. A proven method to begin a discussion is to ask your children their opinions. It makes them reflect, feel important and involved. You will find most children are very honest when giving their opinions. The conversation should begin with emphasis on the positive. What was accomplished? What was learned? Ask your child if there was feedback he/she found upsetting. Ask why it was upsetting. The challenge is to discuss all feedback in a manner that promotes the needed results without being overly critical. Always be sensitive to your children's feelings. When you actively listen, you will be surprised at all you will learn about your children.

Encourage your child to share with you whatever information he/she receives from their teachers. When you review grades ask him/her how he/she feels about the grade and any teacher's comments. Encourage your child to discuss the "why" behind the grade and/or comment. What compliments need to be fully appreciated? What remedies need to be tried? You child owns the work. This is how you teach your child to be responsible for his/her own achievements. Use this discussion to identify your child's strengths and weaknesses and to assist him/her to make plans for improvement. Let your child take the lead in defining how

A PATH TO LEARNING AND LITERACY

to improve studying while you provide guidance and encouragement.

When you review the teachers' comments on your child's work it is important to view it with objectivity. You know your child and his/her ability and level of work. What is the teacher trying to say? How is your child understanding and reacting to the comment? Do you need to jointly discuss the comment or is he/she capable of comprehending the teachers' suggestions?

This familiarity with your child's performance will serve you well during parent/teacher conferences. You and the teacher are members of the same team in supporting your child. You each have unique knowledge to share with each other of how to help your child improve. Remember the teacher sees your child in a completely different environment and will offer another perspective into his/her abilities and work habits. As a parent it is important for you to actively listen and confirm your understanding of the teacher's message. Your child will be anxious to hear about the conference. Be sure to share what you have learned with him/her.

The skill of listening is ongoing. Practice it daily by talking about a TV show, or a sports' game. Hear what your child has to say on a variety of topics. Compliment his/her opinions. Keep the feedback upbeat and positive. Carry the practice over to asking you child what he/she did in school. Remember, each new unit and each new assignment or project needs to be understood to be completed at a mastery level. Each time your child applies active listening skills and shares

A PATH TO LEARNING AND LITERACY

information and ideas with others he/she builds content knowledge and the ability to do outstanding work. Each time your child uses the feedback he/she receives to make adjustments and modifications in his/her work, he/she is raising the personal learning bar.

A PATH TO LEARNING AND LITERACY

Chapter 5
LEARNING

A PATH TO LEARNING AND LITERACY

Chapter 5 Learning:

How do you acquire new information?

> **Learning takes many forms.**
> **Learners use the learning tools.**

We all learn something new every day. We learn by our past experiences and by new opportunities. We go to school to learn. In school we gain a body of knowledge that will help us become better informed about many topics. But how do we learn? We all learn in different ways and use a variety of tools to help us learn. Learning is discovering and it requires discipline.

If you followed the suggestions offered, you already know when and where you will study as well as how to identify the tasks before you begin. Learning new information requires concentration and explanation. When you receive new information in class you should review that information and reinforce that knowledge by doing the assigned homework. Be sure to use the verbalizing skills from Chapter 2 and the previewing techniques from Chapter 3 to prepare for learning the content. When learning new information, you should keep a sheet of paper handy to jot down any key words (see Study Guides Section 4) or ideas and make note any items you are not sure of. Knowing what you do not know is a key to gaining the correct knowledge and increasing your learning.

A PATH TO LEARNING AND LITERACY

The tools of learning are textbooks, assignment pads/agenda books, notebooks, and supplementary materials such as handouts and web sites that can be kept in your notebook. Computers and cell phones will give you access to the internet as needed.

Textbooks contain a body of knowledge and have an organizational plan. They all have a Tables of Contents, a Glossary, and an Index. Learn to use these textbook resources. In the Table of Contents, you will find the page listings for chapters and the sub-headings of a chapter. The Table of Contents assists you in finding information by topic or locating illustrations or other graphics. Take the time to PREVIEW (see Chapter 3) the Table of Contents in your textbook. It contains a wealth of information. The textbook contains content specific vocabulary. These vocabulary terms are listed and defined in the glossary. Use the glossary to learn the definitions of the words that explain the content. Finally, use the index to locate the words, names, or other key terms within the body of the text. The index will give you the pages where a specific name or term can be found. When you understand key words and terms and how they are used in a specific subject context you are demonstrating your ability to learn, and you are increasing your ability to make inferences and draw conclusions. By increasing your vocabulary, you increase your potential for greater achievement – in specific content knowledge, in general understanding and in taking tests.

In textbooks each chapter has a plan of organization. You should become familiar with it. Notice the key terms and

A PATH TO LEARNING AND LITERACY

facts emphasized with italics or bold-faced print. Review the main ideas in the summary at the end of the chapter to reinforce your understanding of the content.

If you are using worksheets that correspond to a textbook, be sure you are working with the correct chapter and chapter section in the text. It is important to read the directions on a worksheet and not assume you know what is expected. Remember you want to work smart as noted in Chapter 3.

Assignment pads or agenda books are essential learning tools. They are your daily planners. You must get in the habit of dating your entries and writing your homework assignments in complete detail. Too many students take shortcuts in copying assignments and they do not know what is required. Therefore, they don't know how or what to study. You should always be able to go back to your assignment pad to get clarification of what you are supposed to do.

Notebooks are essential learning tools that will be your most important asset in studying. It takes time and effort to create and keep a complete and organized notebook. Your teacher may or may not require one, but you should get in the habit of keeping one.

Establish the pattern of dating all your notes. This is a first step in keeping it organized. It is your record of what is taught and when. If you are absent, you will know which days' notes you are missing. Be sure to get those notes as soon as possible. In your notebook you may want to create different sections for class notes, vocabulary, graphics, handouts, website addresses, and completed assignments. You should also keep all returned tests, either in your notebook or in a folder.

Keeping a well-organized and complete notebook will give you a sense of satisfaction and you will have created a magnificent learning tool that will be invaluable in your studying. Get into the habit of routinely reviewing your notebook because research has proven that understanding and retention of content more than doubles if you review the information within 24 hours of being taught that information.

Modeling and Webbing are two instructional strategies that help you learn. They are methods to visually illustrate information. When you see them on the board in the classroom or in a textbook you should notice the patterns, relationships, or examples they are demonstrating.

Modeling is learning by example and is a proven method of effective learning. If you want to learn something new, such as a math theory, look at the model given in the textbook. Work the model through step-by-step to its conclusion. When you do this carefully, you will realize what you know and understand. Where you have questions and need clarification, make a note to ask your teacher to go over the information. Another way of learning is to use the model to analyze the process; start from the solution to a problem and work backwards to gain insights into the process being described.

A PATH TO LEARNING AND LITERACY

Webbing is a visual learning tool that organizes topical information and shows the connections between concepts and ideas. It will help you highlight key information and distinguish between main ideas and supporting details. Webbing can include Concept Maps, Cause and Effect Charts, Venn Diagrams, and other illustrations. It is amazing how much we learn by seeing (visual learning). See the diagram below that illustrates some Tools of Learning. The main idea or focus of the web is Learning Tools; the surrounding examples of learning tools are Assignment Pads, Textbooks, Notebooks, Modeling and Webbing.

There are many ways to learn. Learn how you learn and apply those strategies to building your learning style.

A PATH TO LEARNING AND LITERACY

FREQUENTLY ASKED QUESTIONS

- **What is meant by using discipline to learn?** Discipline refers to establishing personal routines for doing assignments. Preparing homework and reviewing classroom work on a regular basis is the best way to excel in a subject.

- **What is meant by KNOWING WHAT YOU DON'T KNOW?** When you realize there is information that you do not understand, you become aware of the questions you must ask and the topics you must devote more time to studying.

- **What are the tools for learning?** Tools for learning are textbooks, notes, assignment pads/agenda books, notebooks, computer programs, websites and other materials that help you stay organized and understand information.

- **Why is vocabulary so important?** Knowing the meaning of words helps you understand the larger body of knowledge. Vocabulary also helps you to draw conclusions and make inferences.

- **Do I really need to read the textbook?** Yes, but the key is to learn how to read and use a subject specific textbook. It is used to gain initial knowledge and then as a resource for checking specific information and facts. You may want to recheck previewing techniques as noted in Chapter 3.

A PATH TO LEARNING AND LITERACY

➢ **Assignment pads, again?** How you keep your assignment pad or agenda book is a window into your ability to stay current with your schoolwork.

➢ **Why is a notebook so important?** Notebooks are a compilation of everything you are studying on a specific subject. You organize the content of your notebook according to your needs. Because you create the notebook, you are reinforcing all the knowledge you are learning.

➢ **How does modeling and webbing help me to learn?** These are two learning strategies that help you organize and visualize information. They give you another way to see and understand information.

➢ **How do I learn, "how I learn?"** Pay attention to the lessons in class and become aware of how you enjoy learning. Listening: do you hear what is being taught and remember it? Recording: do you have to take notes and write down the information to remember and learn it? Visualizing: sometimes it helps you to see something to understand it, such as in modeling or webbing. We all learn in a variety of different ways. It will not take you very long to realize which of your five senses you use to learn.

A PATH TO LEARNING AND LITERACY

CHAPTER CHECK UP

Check your understanding.

Answer the following questions:
- Do I make connections between discovering and learning?
- Do I keep a running subject vocabulary list?
- Do I know my tools of learning?
- Am I aware of how to read my textbook and use its resources?
- Is my notebook organized and complete?
- What is the best way for me to learn?

Check your progress.

Apply these strategies.
- Recognize how you are discovering and learning.
- Read and use your textbook as a learning tool.
- Understand the vocabulary associated with the subject.
- Keep a well-organized notebook.
- Apply a variety of learning strategies and senses to help you understand new information.

A PATH TO LEARNING AND LITERACY

Checklist

Advance your progress. Use this checklist to check how well you are applying learning skills.
- ➢ *I am listening attentively in class.*
- ➢ *I accurately record my homework assignments.*
- ➢ *I am taking all class notes as instructed.*
- ➢ *I am using illustrations, concept maps, modeling, and webbing to help me learn.*
- ➢ *I know how to use my textbook effectively.*
- ➢ *I keep a well-organized notebook.*
- ➢ *I am having fun while learning.*

A PATH TO LEARNING AND LITERACY

A NOTE TO PARENTS

Parents and teachers are partners in helping children learn. Therefore, parents need to be aware of what their children are learning. Currently with all children participating with online instruction in the home, parents are more aware of the rigorous demands in the classrooms. It is important to continue this awareness when there is the opportunity to attend curriculum sessions for parents; be sure to take advantage of them. This is a major reason for curriculum nights during the traditional school year. During these information events the teachers will review and explain the curriculum and the requirements a student is expected to fulfill in the course. Parents should make every attempt to attend these programs. The curriculum nights/events give you a good idea of what your children are learning, and your children will be proud to know you are taking an active role in their education.

As you assist your children in establishing routines, pay attention to how they learn. Some will learn best by listening, some by observing, and some by doing. We all use a variety of these styles to learn, but we tend to favor one way. Notice what your children enjoy doing while they are working on projects and homework. Then encourage them to build on their learning strengths.

It is important to help your children identify the tools of learning and how to use them. When you receive the supply list at the beginning of the school term jointly review it and plan an outing with your children to purchase the needed supplies.

A PATH TO LEARNING AND LITERACY

Don't forget the assignment pad/agenda book and the notebooks.

Be sure to pay attention to the learning tools that are supplied by the school - specifically, textbooks. Textbooks need to be valued and used on a routine basis by students. Help your children become familiar with their textbooks and how to use them. You may want to remind them to Preview the reading assignments in their textbook. (See Chapter 3)

Some courses provide text material on hand-out sheets. Encourage you students to keep these papers organized by putting them in sequential order and place them in a folder. Also, tell your child to date each of these pages when he/she receives them.

Keeping an organized and complete notebook is a key to learning. Help your children set up their notebooks and take the time to review them regularly. This will keep you current on what your children are learning and how well they are staying organized. You can also discuss the contents of the notebook with your children, ask them to explain their notes and help reinforce their learning.

When you review your children's notebooks you become aware of the subject content and the use of learning tools such as content mapping or recommended websites that supplement learning. You are an active partner in your children's education.

Chapter 6
STUDYING

A PATH TO LEARNING AND LITERACY

Chapter 6   Studying:

How do you go about studying?

> **Identify what to study.**
> **Learn different ways to study.**

Studying is a learned skill; it is how you reinforce learning. Studying strategies will be as individualized as your learning strategies but there are some basics. Studying involves using a variety of resources. Examine the web below to determine the different items you could use in studying.

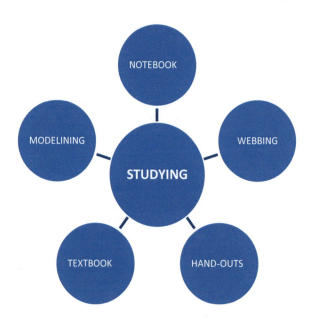

A PATH TO LEARNING AND LITERACY

How would you use each of these learning tools in your studying? They all contribute to your knowledge of the subject matter. Are there any additional tools you would add to this list? What are they? How do they help you study? Add them to your list of study tools.

When the goal of your studying is to reinforce what you have learned in class, you need a daily review of your notebook and what was done in class. This is always a good idea. Therefore, get in the habit of reviewing your notebooks, class notes, vocabulary, and hand-out materials – as part of your regular routine. Research has proven that understanding and retention of content more than doubles if you review the information within 24 hours of being taught.

It is extremely helpful to review your textbook after you have learned a new lesson. The content of the textbook will be easier to understand than when you originally read it, and by reviewing your textbook you will be using visual learning to reinforce your knowledge of the subject.

When you work on written assignments, be sure to refer to the checklists in **Chapter 3 Process** and complete all the essential details listed in the homework assignment. If you have written assignments that require you to reference your notebook materials, you will appreciate the value of a well-organized and complete notebook.

Homework serves the purpose of practicing what was taught in class. Assigning homework to reinforce class instruction is a strategy used by most teachers. Doing homework helps build your knowledge and confidence of the subject matter.

Sometimes homework will prepare you for the next day's lesson. You should look at this type of homework as a preview of what is to come. Give careful attention to details and if there is anything you don't fully understand you should ask questions in class the following day to clarify the homework.

Whether homework is done to review information or learn new information it is a valuable and important part of studying. When you complete your homework, you will be prepared for class. The confidence of knowing what is being taught will increase your attention span and your understanding of the topic.

Studying to test your knowledge of a topic or unit of study requires a different approach. You need to make a plan that includes what to study, how much time you will need and which techniques to use.

When you are studying for a major test you make a concentrated effort to master a specific body of knowledge. The following steps will help you focus your efforts.

- ➢ Identify the specific topics that will be included in the test.

A PATH TO LEARNING AND LITERACY

> ➢ Assemble the information that supports what you have learned on those topics.

This information will include ...

- *Specific pages in your textbook*
- *Notebook*
    - *Class notes*
    - *Handouts*
    - *Graphics, Modeling, Webbing*
    - *Other related information in your notebook*
- *Homework assignments.*

Once you have identified your resources and all the information you are responsible for studying and knowing, you need to decide on a study procedure. The following suggestions are effective study strategies:

- Reciting – Read your notes and other materials aloud. This allows you to hear the information while reading it. You are studying orally and visually.

- Teaching – You could teach the information to someone else, a friend or a parent or teach it to yourself.

- Study Tricks – Look for connections in content then design personal learning tools for remembering formulas or a series of related items. These are called mnemonic devices. (See Frequently Asked Questions for an example) You can also use study charts. (See Study Guides Section)

- Practice Sample Questions – This will help you become aware of how questions are worded. Keep the answers handy so you can check the accuracy of your responses.

- Summarizing – Write the information in your own words in lists or in paragraphs. You can also use index cards to create flash cards. (See Study Guides Section)

- Drilling – Repeat information by saying it aloud or by writing it down until you know it. This is helpful with learning spelling words, vocabulary words, and mathematics and science formulas.

When studying for a test you should know the format of the test you will be taking. The basic testing formats are short answer questions and written responses or essays. Short answer questions can be multiple choice, fill-in, matching, true/false, etc. All short answer questions focus on factual information, and basic understanding. When you are preparing for a short answer test you need to practice your understanding of the content specifics and vocabulary. An essay exam or extended response requires you to plan your answer. You do this by listing the items you need to write about, identifying details and examples to include, organizing your ideas, drawing conclusions, and then writing your essay using an introduction, body, and conclusion. Be sure to check that you have answered the question and given supportive details.

You should practice answering the type of questions you will see on the exam. This will help you understand the content information and will also build your confidence in becoming familiar with the questioning techniques. Be sure to take the time to carefully read all questions. You should practice writing an essay in preparation for an essay exam. Allow yourself a specified amount of time to write the practice essay because when you take a test you need to include all the important information and complete the writing task within a specified time. Practice makes it easier and less stressful.

Finally, after you've done all your studying, be sure to get a good night's sleep and eat a good breakfast before going to class. This will help you be alert and ready to do your best. A car needs fuel to operate, you need sleep and food to do your best.

A PATH TO LEARNING AND LITERACY

Frequently Asked Questions

> ### What is the difference between learning and studying?
> Learning is acquiring new information and studying is reviewing that information until you have mastered it.

> ### Is doing homework a form of studying?
> Yes, when you do homework to reinforce and review what you've done in class you are studying that information. Homework can also be learning when you are preparing for a new unit of study. For example, you read a section in your textbook that the teacher will discuss in class the next day.

> ### What tools do I need to study for a major test?
> This will vary, but you should have your notebook and textbook to start. Make a checklist of what tools were used while you were learning the material and those are the tools you should include in your studying.

> ### Why do I need to know the types of questions that will be on a test?
> Answering different questions requires different skills. In short answer questions where choices are given, you need to identify key words and make connections. In extended response questions you'll need to write your answers based on your knowledge and supply your own examples.

A PATH TO LEARNING AND LITERACY

- **Do I need to use all the study strategies?** You should use as many different strategies to study as possible. The more senses you use, the more involved you are in studying.

- **What are mnemonic devices?** They are a shortcut method to learning lists or procedures. One method is to use the first letter of each item you need to know and make a new word or create a silly sentence using first letters of words. For example: The Causes of WWI were Nationalism, Imperialism, Militarism and the System of Alliances or **NIMS.**

- **Is practicing answering questions that important in studying?** Yes! You do not want any surprises when you are taking a test. By becoming familiar with how questions are worded you increase your questioning vocabulary and you also are studying the content.

- **Why do I need a good night's sleep before a test?** Taking a test requires you to be alert and focused. You need to think clearly and do your best. Your brain and your body work best when they are fully charged with a good night's sleep. And don't forget to eat a good breakfast.

A PATH TO LEARNING AND LITERACY

CHAPTER CHECK UP

Check Your Understanding

Answer the following questions.
- Do I know what to study?
- Do I know how I learn best?
- Do I read my assignment/notes aloud?
- Do I read my class notes when I get home from school?
- Do I diagram a problem or issue by using a concept map or web?
- Do I have all the information I need to study for an exam?
- Have I designed any mnemonic devices to help me study?
- Do I maintain a complete notebook?

Check Your Progress

Apply these strategies.
- Know what and how to study.
- Use all the learning tools available.
- Review all information daily.
- Use your various senses and different approaches to learning.
- Maintain a comprehensive notebook.

A PATH TO LEARNING AND LITERACY

Checklist

Advance your progress. Use this checklist to increase your studying skills.
- ➤ I identify the relevant pages in the textbook.
- ➤ I organize and review all handouts.
- ➤ I maintain a complete notebook.
- ➤ I learn subject specific vocabulary words.
- ➤ I use different learning strategies to demonstrate greater understanding.
- ➤ I schedule enough time to complete an assignment and to study for a test.
- ➤ I feel confident when I'm finished studying.

A PATH TO LEARNING AND LITERACY

A Note to Parents

Be aware that the process of actual studying can be extremely stressful for your child. The emphasis put on developing routine practices is a way to reduce this stress. Encourage your child to make studying an ongoing routine so they will not be overwhelmed when a test arrives.

It is important to look at your child's notebooks. Spend some time to help your child keep his/her notebooks organized and complete. All children need to be taught how to keep things in order and need to learn to appreciate the importance of keeping papers and other information for an extended period of time.

When you become acquainted with your child's schedule, you will have an idea of when tests will be given or when projects are due. You should put these important dates on an appointment calendar. By modeling organization and planning you are setting a wonderful example for your child.

Children need to learn how to study for themselves. Your role is to provide gentle reminders and be available when asked or needed. If your child is in the habit of routinely preparing homework and does a thorough job on homework, it will be easier to prepare for an exam. As a resource person, your role is to focus you child's efforts on what to study for the test and how much time he/she will need to study. You could also ask them, how they plan to study for an exam and together design a schedule.

A PATH TO LEARNING AND LITERACY

As parents you should become acquainted with the types of exams your children are taking. Discuss with your children the various types of questions they can be asked on a test and listen to their strategies for studying and for answering questions. Finally, encourage your children to practice answering questions.

Above all encourage an atmosphere where learning is exciting and rewarding with a minimum of stress.

A PATH TO LEARNING AND LITERACY

SECTION 3 ACCOMPLISHMENT

Chapter 7 – Evaluation
Chapter 8 – Achievement
Chapter 9 – Celebration

Chapter 7
EVALUATION

Chapter 7 Evaluation:

How is your academic performance?

> *Evaluation is a continuous process.*
> *Evaluation is an essential learning tool.*

Evaluation is the process of reviewing your work to determine your progress in learning. It is an important part of learning. Doing well in school is everyones' dream even if we don't always admit it. Realistically, doing well is a continuous challenge. Learning requires identifying information and then finding ways to understand and absorb that information. Evaluation indicates the extent of your success in mastering information.

When you analyze the feedback you receive, you identify your own strengths as well as the areas where you need improvement. Initially, you evaluate your homework when you check to see that you've completed all the requirements and double checked it for accuracy. When you ask your parents and/or friends to check over your assignments, you listen to what they say and evaluate their comments. Your teachers evaluate your work when they give you feedback in the form of a grade or through comments. It is important for you to pay attention to your teacher's feedback. It is a source of continually improving the quality of your work.

Throughout a unit of study, the feedback you get on homework and class work gives you insights into your understanding of the material and content. Pay attention to this feedback. Teachers want to help you succeed. You should ask them to explain any directions or suggestions you do not understand. When you ask questions, it makes you an active participant in learning.

Test results should also be evaluated. Good scores make you feel good. They confirm what you are doing correctly. They provide reinforcement for you to continue the successful path you've been following. Congratulate yourself on a job well done, but also consider why and how you did well. Make note of what worked well for you. Write yourself that additional comment or add a star to the grade to show how proud you are of your performance. Poor grades can make you feel frustrated. They can make you feel discouraged and cause you to lack confidence in yourself and your abilities. DON'T GIVE POOR SCORES THIS POWER!!! Learn to use them to your advantage.

Too often when students receive a poor grade on a test, they hide it among school stuff and want to forget it exists. Students who do this are doing themselves a great disservice. Everyone learns from their mistakes. How do you turn a poor grade into a positive learning experience? If you do poorly on a test, try to figure out why by asking yourself these questions:

A PATH TO LEARNING AND LITERACY

> ➢ *Did I study enough?*
> ➢ *Did I know what to study?*
> ➢ *Did I study the correct information?*
> ➢ *Did I read the test questions carefully?*
> ➢ *What kind of mistakes did I make?*
> ➢ *How can I correct these mistakes?*
> ➢ *How can I improve the preparation for my next test?*

The answers to these questions will provide valuable insights into your own personal learning style. Take the time to reflect on your answers to determine why you received a poor grade. Knowing what you now know, what could you have done differently to improve your grade? Make notes for future reference.

When you receive a grade you're unhappy with, you must calm yourself down. It is natural to become defensive and try to blame someone or something for your poor performance. Once you calm yourself down you can begin to examine why you received the grade you did. Get out a piece of paper and write down your observations. Use the questions listed above to start. Continue the process by looking at the questions you got wrong and identify the correct answer. Why did you put the answer you gave? This will give you insights into your reasoning while you were taking the test.

When you finish reviewing the test, you should be able to answer the question – how could I have done better on this exam? Now discuss this with your parents and/or your teacher. It is amazing how verbalizing these observations will help you to improve your performance in the future. This is so important! Do not skip talking about what you've learned

A PATH TO LEARNING AND LITERACY

about your performance with your parents and/or your teachers. All learning is reinforced by using as many of your senses as possible. This is true for rediscovering how you learn.

Evaluation is a continuous process and you will want to keep a record of your personal growth. You can do this by reviewing all suggestions for improvement. Review your notes on what has worked on tests and homework assignments. Pay careful attention to what you learn about improving your studying strategies and/or answering questions on a test. These are the strategies and techniques you should routinely apply in doing homework and taking tests. Stay positive! Enjoy the feeling of satisfaction in knowing that you are using evaluation as an essential learning tool to improve your performance. Remember when something works use it to your advantage.

A PATH TO LEARNING AND LITERACY

Frequently Asked Questions

- **What is evaluation?** – *Evaluation is a method of measuring your academic performance. It can be in the form of grades and/or comments. It is ongoing and does not stop once you've received a test grade.*

- **What is feedback?** – *This is other people's reaction to your work. It can be in the form of comments and grades. All evaluation is a form of feedback.*

- **Why evaluate feedback?** – *When you take the time to review comments and reasons for your grades you learn how to improve your performance. By evaluating feedback, you are discovering specific strengths and weaknesses in your performance and your studying.*

- **How should I react to a poor grade?** – *Calm down and analyze why you did poorly? All grades should be used as learning experiences. Review the questions in this chapter on how to improve a poor grade and take the necessary steps to do better next time.*

- **Where should I keep my old tests and homework assignments?** – *Design a system to keep you papers throughout the term. You could keep them in a section in your notebook or in a separate*

A PATH TO LEARNING AND LITERACY

folder. Use these resources to review, study and monitor your improvement and growth.

➤ **Why do I need to verbalize what I learn about my grades?** – *It has been proven that the more senses you use in the learning process, the stronger the learning. Verbalizing makes you say and hear your plan to improve. Discussing how to implement your plan builds a personal sense of commitment to improve.*

➤ **Why be positive?** *When you have a positive attitude, people will recognize your willingness to listen to suggestions for improvement. It shows you are taking responsibility for your learning. Another way of understanding what being positive means is the famous saying "the glass is half full."*

A PATH TO LEARNING AND LITERACY

CHAPTER CHECK UP

Check Your Understanding

Answer the following questions:
- ➢ Did I study enough?
- ➢ Did I study the correct information?
- ➢ Did I know what to study?
- ➢ Did I read the test questions carefully?
- ➢ What types of mistakes did I make?
- ➢ How can I correct these mistakes?
- ➢ How can I improve the preparation for my next test?

Check Your Progress

Apply these strategies.
- ➢ Review feedback for suggestions.
- ➢ Identify information that needs correction.
- ➢ Take active steps to understand how you learn.
- ➢ Keep a file of your written work.
- ➢ Monitor your progress.
- ➢ Stay positive.

Checklist

Advance your progress by checking your answers to these questions.
- ➢ What is my score?
- ➢ How do I feel about the score?
- ➢ Do I understand how I received the score?
- ➢ Is there room for improvement?
- ➢ How can I improve?
- ➢ Did I verbalize to someone the steps on how I can improve?
- ➢ When will I begin to take these steps to improve?
- ➢ Did I file my work/test for future reference?

A PATH TO LEARNING AND LITERACY

A Note to Parents

Parents want their children to feel good about their schoolwork. Whatever emotions your children feel, you feel that emotion to a greater degree. You are thrilled with their successes and worried about their problems. Knowing how to help your children have a positive attitude toward school is an ongoing challenge for parents. The process of analyzing feedback and staying emotionally detached is another challenge for all parents. Teachers and Parents are both advocates for student success. Therefore, teachers' comments should be viewed as suggestions for how to improve. Encourage your children to share their teachers' comments with you and discuss them together. These include comments on homework, projects, and tests.

Encouraging your children to analyze their test results is a way for them to understand how and why they did well, as well as how they can improve. Evaluation and analysis are high level thinking skills and require your help and guidance to be successful. If test scores and feedback are good, take the time to recognize why. Give positive comments on grades and specific answers. This reinforces positive achievement.

When the results are not satisfactory, remember your children feel terrible bringing home a poor grade and they need your compassionate understanding, not more criticism. Very delicately, walk your children through the analytical process and reassure them of your confidence in their abilities. Review the work together and take note of where mistakes were made and why. Identify the steps that need to be taken to avoid

A PATH TO LEARNING AND LITERACY

those mistakes in the future. When you are dealing with pre-school or elementary school age children, it is the parents who will have to take the lead in this process of examining results.

With older children poor grades can sometimes fall through the cracks. It is important for parents to keep a continuous dialogue with their children about schoolwork. Don't be judgmental, be open to discussion! Ask your children about their homework and test scores and listen to their comments about how they are doing. This will give you an idea of whether you need to dig deeper into their academic performance.

Most schools have numerous methods for establishing relationships between home and school. There are Back-to-School Curriculum Programs for parents, quarterly report cards, parent conferences, teacher phone calls, written notices of poor performance and some type of failure alert. Schools have online resources for checking progress and promoting constant communication between home and school. Find out about the Parent Portal in your child's school. It is your responsibility to be aware of these online offerings. As parents you need to know how your children are doing and have insights into their performance. Welcome all communication with school as a resource for knowing more about your child's performance. View your conversations, texts, and emails with your child's teachers as sources of feedback. Parents and teachers working together create the successful student.

A PATH TO LEARNING AND LITERACY

Chapter 8
ACHIEVEMENT

A PATH TO LEARNING AND LITERACY

Chapter 8 Achievement:

What have you accomplished?

> Be a cheerleader!
> Success takes
> discipline, discovery, and determination!

Achievement is the knowledge that you are making progress toward reaching a goal. You have been working long and hard and you should be feeling a sense of satisfaction in what you have been doing. In a perfect world everyone would get A+ and be on the honor role, but the real world is quite different. It is important to learn to be good to yourself and not be overly critical of your own accomplishments. Resist the impulse to become easily frustrated when you're not satisfied with your results. Instead, take the time to reflect and take inventory of the progress you have made. You may not see the improvements as fast as you would like to, but good habits will make a difference over time. Recognize the positive in what you have accomplished. Success is measured by the steps you take toward achieving your goal.

The following is a list of achievements that will give you a feeling of accomplishment. You owe it to yourself to take the time to reflect on the positive things you have done and be proud of yourself. Give yourself credit for your accomplishments along the way!

- You completed your assignments on time! **Good start!**

- You reviewed a test and made corrections! **Making Progress!**

- You realized how you could improve your test taking skills! **You gained important insights!**

- You spoke with others about how you're doing and listened to their advice! **That shows self-discipline and responsibility!**

Remember to be your own cheerleader. The encouragement that you give yourself will help you continue to strive and excel. Success does not happen overnight. It is a cumulative process that takes discipline, discovery, and determination.

What successes should you acknowledge? Throughout the book you've learned how to discipline yourself in establishing work habits and study routines. It is difficult to sit down to do homework at a given time and place, but it will deliver results. If you have done that, congratulate yourself on following a routine! When you complete an assignment and you have that 'feel good' feeling of a job well done; that is a form of a reward. Congratulate yourself on your effort and your sense of self-satisfaction! You may want to keep a tally on your calendar when assignments are completed on time and you have stuck to your study schedule. This will help you visualize your progress. See how many continuous homework assignments you can prepare on schedule. When you've done

A PATH TO LEARNING AND LITERACY

a week's worth of assignments on time treat yourself to something you like! Do something you enjoy! You will be amazed how much you enjoy something when you know you've earned it. You are becoming your own cheerleader!

Think about the other skills you have learned to focus on. How to actively listen; how to become better organized; how to study; how to review results; how to work toward achieving your goals. These are major efforts and wonderful accomplishments! Be proud of the self-discipline you displayed in applying these learning strategies!

You found ways to adjust your work habits and/or study habits because you have gained insights into what works for you. This is certainly something you should recognize. It means you believe in your ability to continually improve. It shows maturity and self-knowledge and is a source of major growth.

An effective way to acknowledge your progress is to keep a record of your performance. Record your score, the difference (positive and negative) from the previous score, and any comments for improvement. Include scores and comments on your homework, tests, and projects. Your motivation to continually improve will be stimulated by visually depicting your progress.

Finally, share the good news! When you feel happy with what you've accomplished, you'll be amazed how happy you can make others feel by sharing your experiences with them. Share your feelings with those who helped you along the way – your parents and your teachers, maybe a friend. They will be happy to share in your sense of achievement. Share your disappointments as well. You will be amazed at the insights other people can offer. Challenge yourself to turn your disappointments into accomplishments.

A PATH TO LEARNING AND LITERACY

Frequently Asked Questions

- ***What is meant by achievement?*** *Achievement is when you are making progress. It is a way to measure your improvement and to feel good about your effort.*

- ***Why should I recognize my accomplishments?*** *Each accomplishment represents a forward step you've taken toward reaching your goal. That is an achievement and congratulations are in order.*

- ***How do I learn to become my own cheerleader?*** *Recognize the positive things you do in improving your study habits. Appreciate the hard work you have put in and know that you've earned your rewards. Enjoy rewarding yourself.*

- ***How do I achieve success?*** *Success happens in stages. Each chapter in this book has addressed a step toward success. If you have applied what you've learned you are taking steps on your individual PATH TO LEARNING AND LITERACY. You are discovering what works for you. This experience will lead to self-discovery; you will learn how to reinvent what you are doing to achieve YOUR PERSONAL SUCCESS STORY.*

A PATH TO LEARNING AND LITERACY

- ➢ **How should I reward myself?** *Tell yourself that you are doing a good job. Enjoy that feeling of accomplishment. Know that you have earned a reward that reflects your level of accomplishment. Give yourself a special treat.*

- ➢ **Why should I keep a record of my progress?** *This is a way to validate your effort and your accomplishments. You will learn which studying strategies work the best for you. You will visually see your progress.*

A PATH TO LEARNING AND LITERACY

CHAPTER CHECK UP

Check Your Understanding

Answer the following questions.
- How much progress have I made?
- Have my study habits improved?
- Have my test scores improved?
- Do I have more confidence in my abilities?
- Do I reward myself when I do well in school?
- Do I share my successes with other people?
- Am I keeping a record of my achievement?
- Am I my own cheerleader?

Check Your Progress

Apply these strategies.
- Recognize your achievements step by step.
- Make a list of the improvements you've noticed in yourself.
- Realize the effort you've applied in doing school-work.
- Adjust your study habits to reflect your individual style.
- Feel good about your improvements.
- Reward yourself.
- Share you sense of accomplishment with others.

A PATH TO LEARNING AND LITERACY

Checklist

Advance your progress. Use this checklist to measure your achievement.

- ➢ *My homework habits have improved.*
- ➢ *I'm improving my study skills.*
- ➢ *I'm keeping track of my academic progress.*
- ➢ *I know how I've improved and what I still must work on.*
- ➢ *I can make adjustments in my studying habits to meet my needs.*
- ➢ *I recognize my improvements and reward myself.*
- ➢ *I share my success with others.*

A PATH TO LEARNING AND LITERACY

A Note to Parents

As previously stated, parents are their children's first and most important teachers. Therefore, your children look to you to validate their accomplishments. They want to please you. When you offer recognition for their effort and work, it is a great motivation.

It is essential to recognize children's achievements on a regular and most times on a daily basis. Visually show how proud you are as a family of your children's achievements. Outwardly demonstrating that pride is a wonderful boost to your child's ego. Here are some suggestions for ways to show how proud you are of your child.

- ➢ The refrigerator is decorated with the preschoolers or early childhood student's papers. How wonderful! Should this stop with elementary school?

- ➢ The parent who has a kind word for a child who is working hard does as much to lift his/her spirits as the high grade. Be sure to always be sincere. Children need and want honesty.

- ➢ Listening to your child talk about what he/she has done and how he/she feels about schoolwork makes it that much more meaningful. Children love to know you listen to them!

- ➢ Surprising your children with a small token of appreciation gives them an enormous sense of importance. It tells them you've been thinking about them.

> Be a cheerleader for your children. It is with your support that they can confidently take risks and face challenges.

> Help your children keep records of their progress. Together you can identify the benchmarks that you'll want to recognize and celebrate.

Taking the time to recognize your children's achievements is a way for you to become aware of the progress they have made. Improving personal learning strategies is a demanding and slow process. Your children will become frustrated and need your encouragement along the way. Your compliments are the motivation that keep your children working. Notice if they are doing their homework on a regular basis without your prompting. Be sure to compliment them on that. Notice where your kids are applying themselves, such as effectively using their study time, organizing their materials, improving their study skills, analyzing their test scores. Use examples of their positive improvement to discuss how proud you are of them.

When your children know and feel you care and how much you are concerned for them, it will make them work even harder. Your children notice how you recognize their accomplishments and it builds their self-esteem. When your children know you listen to them it gives them the confidence to talk with you and not be judged. You are on the same side! You are someone they can trust, and you are their Cheerleader.

A PATH TO LEARNING AND LITERACY

A PATH TO LEARNING AND LITERACY

Chapter 9
CELEBRATION

A PATH TO LEARNING AND LITERACY

Chapter 9 Celebration:

Are you ready to celebrate?

> **Celebrate, you deserve it!**
> **Take inventory of your successes!**

Celebration is claiming your reward. Only you know what you gained from exploring and applying the content of this book. Through your efforts you learned new skills and how to appreciate them. You realized some of your potential and seen it demonstrated in the work you created and in what you have accomplished. You have become more aware of your abilities and taken the self-disciplined steps needed to achieve your goal. Definitely, it is time to celebrate.

Celebration is a step beyond achievement. It is a time to recognize your accomplishments and share your successes. To fully celebrate your accomplishments, you should take an inventory of your successes. You may want to draw up a list of your greatest challenges and how you met them. Knowing what you know now, is there anything you would do differently? Write it down for future reference.

Celebration can take many forms.

Students who made advancements in a specific subject or class might receive recognition from their teacher and/or classmates. This may take the form of a certificate or

A PATH TO LEARNING AND LITERACY

award. If you received such an award, be sure to share it with your parents so you can continue the celebration.

Perhaps you have some schoolwork displayed for parents' night or other special events; that is a wonderful thing to celebrate. Be sure to tell your parents to look for your work when they visit. When they come home you can discuss what they saw and their feelings about seeing your work on display. Perhaps you can go together to see the exhibit.

You can choose to participate in competitions ranging from the classroom to the school and beyond. Taking that risk and competing takes courage and is a reason to celebrate. If you receive recognition for that effort, that is a further reason for celebration.

Report Card time is not only for reflection, but celebration! Advancements, no matter how minor, should be recognized and celebrated.

The end of the school year is an especially important milestone in your career. This offers an opportunity to share the highlights of the year with friends and family. Enjoy sharing and celebrating. Do something you have wanted to do. This could range from going somewhere with the special people in your life or receiving an item you have earned by your hard work. Yes, you could even buy something for yourself or request it from your parents.

Make lists of the things you enjoyed doing during the school year and why you enjoyed them. This will give you insights into your future. Make lists of the people you found

A PATH TO LEARNING AND LITERACY

most helpful and how they helped you. You may want to make a point to thank them in some way. Make a list of facts learned that you would always want to *remember*. It will help you build a personal inventory of your interests.

Make a TO DO list of techniques or things you still need to learn. Remember, learning is a lifelong process; there will always be a challenge for you to rise and meet.

At this time, we have all witnessed the creativity that can go into celebration. Society has met the challenge of how to celebrate in 2020. Graduations, proms, sporting events have been reimaged and transformed into virtual events. Technology allows celebrations to be transmitted to loved ones near and far. Yes, celebrating is essential to who we are; to express our personal satisfaction, our accomplishments, our appreciation for others, our sharing our lives with others. So, celebrate!

Celebrate!

You did it!

A PATH TO LEARNING AND LITERACY

Frequently Asked Questions

- **Why celebrate?** You deserve it! It is a way of rewarding yourself for your hard work.

- **Will sharing my achievements with others help me?** Yes, you will realize how important you are to other people and how much they are supporting you.

- **When my work is displayed, is it really a reason for celebration?** By displaying your work your teacher is telling you that your work should be shared with everyone who can see it. You should be extremely proud.

- **Why should I compete?** Competition presents a new challenge to learning. In competitions, you use your personal skills in a different way and face a new challenge. It is a way of accepting more responsibility for your learning.

- **Why do we have report cards?** Report cards are a means of communication between the school and the home. Report cards provide feedback and evaluation and they are a source for reflection and growth.

A PATH TO LEARNING AND LITERACY

➢ ***Why should I do an inventory of my successes?*** *It is important to know what works for you. Doing an inventory of your successes will help you retain the best of your school year. Think of your lists of successes as your own personal yearbook. Your successes will help you get off to a positive start when the next school year begins.*

A PATH TO LEARNING AND LITERACY

CHAPTER CHECK UP

Check Your Understanding

Answer the following questions:
- Do I recognize my own achievements?
- Do others recognize my hard work?
- Have I received any awards or certificates?
- Have I tried entering any competitions?
- Am I happy with my report card grades?
- Do I want to earn something special?
- Have I made an inventory of my successes?

Check Your Progress

Apply these strategies.
- Feel positive about your successes.
- Be proud of Recognitions and Awards.
- Take risks to expand your learning.
- Review Report Cards.
- Make an inventory of your successes.
- Reward your accomplishments.

Checklist

Advance your progress by taking an inventory of your successes in learning.
- What were my greatest challenges and how did I meet them?
- What would I do differently?
- What did I enjoy?
- What did I dislike?
- What will I always remember?
- What do I need to improve?
- What else do I need to learn?

A PATH TO LEARNING AND LITERACY

A Note to Parents

The awesome task of guiding your children in their schoolwork is one of the biggest challenges of parenting. Parents are the coaches who teach their children to become responsible for their own learning. Parents provide the emotional support for their children through the maze of school and homework. Parents, it is your patience and perseverance that serve as a source of strength for your children. Celebrating their successes is truly celebrating your parenting skills.

When your child reaches benchmarks in their studying it is important for you to recognize these achievements. It is a tangible way to show you care and that you are interested in what they do. Teachers will tell you that there is a direct parallel between parental involvement and student success. Be sure to take the time to visit the school on a regular basis – for back-to-school events, concerts, sporting events, special programs, and parent/teacher conferences. Your children's success may depend on it.

Here are some suggestions for ways parents can foster their children's accomplishments and achievements.

- ➢ When your children's work is displayed it is an outward expression of their best efforts and they are yearning for your recognition. Give it the attention it deserves by complimenting them and telling them something specific you liked about their work.

A PATH TO LEARNING AND LITERACY

- Encourage your children to participate in a variety of academic programs as well as enrichment activities. This teaches them strong social skills, encourages them to explore their interests and provides a source for advanced study.

- Support them further by attending any exhibits, concerts, or games they participate in. Your children will welcome the opportunity to discuss these activities when they know they can count on you being there whenever possible.

- Listen to them. This is a way for you to show you truly support them because without saying it, you are encouraging them to express themselves. Children love to be heard.

Be sure to have an ongoing dialogue with your child's teacher(s). If you feel your child has been working especially hard and has not received recognition he/she deserves from the teacher, you should discuss it with the teacher. Do not be afraid to ask the teacher if there is some way your child can be recognized.

The report card is a built-in measure of progress. Your child has carefully analyzed it before giving it to you. Respect that it is an assessment of his/her abilities. Your child owns it and is very much aware that is all about him/her. Ask your child for his/her reactions to the report card grades and/or comments. What he/she says about the grades should be the basis for the discussion you have about the report card. Above

A PATH TO LEARNING AND LITERACY

all, be positive. Pay attention to any improvements that are indicated.

If an improvement is needed ask your child what it is and for suggestions on how to make that improvement. Be sure your child owns the need for improvement and how to accomplish it, as well as owning the progress he has made. Ask your child how he/she deserves to celebrate their Report Card. You will be proud of how honest and sincere he/she is!

Help your child with making the Inventory of Success Lists. Especially at the end of the school year this is a way to sustain the progress he/she has made. These lists will serve as starting points for the following year.

Celebrations and rewards are individual and will vary from family to family. The emphasis should always be on the student. You want to recognize his/her ability to assume responsibility and reward his/her accomplishments.

Guide your children's PATH TO LEARNING AND LITERACY by showing your support and appreciation for the excitement of learning. Encourage a positive learning environment that will be replenished with each new challenge and each new adventure. Showing your children how to learn will reap them a lifetime of rewards.

A PATH TO LEARNING AND LITERACY

A PATH TO LEARNING AND LITERACY

SECTION 4
STUDY GUIDES

An Introduction to Study Guides
  Key Words
  Vocabulary Lists
  Study Charts
  Visual Webs
  Summaries
  Verbalizing

INTRODUCTION TO STUDY GUIDES

Study guides are tools used to master the information you learn in class. They are very individualized and should be adapted to your needs and reflect your learning style. Developing study guides and using them at the conclusion of a unit of study is an excellent way to prepare for an exam.

An important principle to keep in mind when studying is that the more senses that are involved, the more effective the learning. You need to see, hear, speak, write, experience, and perhaps smell the subject matter to master it.

We all learn differently. Some of us are visual learners while others learn best by listening. Some students learn by writing information down while others need to diagram information to help them visualize the connections. Still others like to talk about what they learned. We all learn by employing a variety of these strategies.

As you review the suggestions in this Study Guides Section, you will determine which study technique(s) are best for you. Ideally, after

A PATH TO LEARNING AND LITERACY

reviewing these suggestions you will design your own personal study guide.

The process of creating a personal study guide is a high-level learning activity. The effort you put into creating the guide will be rewarded by automatically increasing your knowledge of the subject matter. It will force you to see more connections in the content. An effective study guide helps everything make sense.

A PATH TO LEARNING AND LITERACY

KEY WORDS

Key Words are the words that give meaning to a unit of study. If you can define and explain the key words in a unit of study, you can be assured that you know the content. Therefore, when you review a unit of study, you need to identify key words such as:

➢ *Names*

➢ *Events*

➢ *Dates*

➢ *Formulas*

➢ *Important facts.*

Make a list of these Key Words to study. It is effective to group the words by category. For example: all names should be on one list, all dates should be on separate list. This helps you to concentrate and focus your studying.

➢ *You could put each word on a separate index card and place an explanation of the Key Word on the reverse side of the card. When you study you can immediately confirm your answer is correct. You can also use your computer to make a two-column chart. Put the key word in one column and the explanation of the key word in the second column. Be sure to keep the key word and explanation carefully aligned. Made a separate two-column chart for each category.*

- *Use the list of key words to explain each section of what you studied. For example: If you were studying geometry principles you could talk about right angles, the hypotenuse, vertical angles, etc.*

- *Use the list of key words to illustrate what you learned by making content maps or webs. (See Visual Webs p. 127)*

- *Practice putting information in sequential order and describing relationships and/or cause and effect.*

A PATH TO LEARNING AND LITERACY

VOCABULARY LISTS

Vocabulary lists are used to help you learn the meanings of new words. There are three types of Vocabulary Lists you should be aware of. They are **new vocabulary words, content vocabulary and questioning vocabulary**.

The first is a list of **new words** you are responsible for learning. Your English teacher may supply a list of words—you will be required to learn the meaning of each word and how to use it in a sentence.

The second type of new vocabulary is **content words**. These are similar to Key Words and are found in the readings you will be doing in class or for homework. They are specific to the topic you are studying. In Social Studies you find new content words when mastered give you a better understanding of the topic. For Example, when you read a selection on - How the United States Expanded Westward - you have to become familiar with vocabulary words such as: manifest destiny, expansion, frontier, wagon trains, pioneer, sod house, annexation, territories. When you learn these

A PATH TO LEARNING AND LITERACY

vocabulary words you will better comprehend the reading selection. It will make sense. You will find the same is true for all subjects. Look for the content vocabulary words related to what you are studying and be sure to know their meanings. Frequently, these words will be in italics. Each subject has words that are unique to that subject. You may find these words listed in the textbook glossary and/or index.

A third type of vocabulary you should be aware of is **question words**. Words, such as list, explain, illustrate, that are found in questions are there to tell you how to answer the question. Look for these words when preparing homework assignments and projects. They are the key to telling you what you are expected to do. When you know the meanings of these words it also helps you in taking tests. Here are some of the questioning words and their meaning. Remember to always ask your teacher to explain a word you don't know the meaning of.

List – *identify two or more items related to a topic.*

Explain – *give a detailed description and reason.*

Illustrate – *give examples that support your ideas.*

A PATH TO LEARNING AND LITERACY

Design – form or sketch an original plan or invent.

Interpret – tell the meaning of something.

Support – give specific examples.

Majority – use more than half.

Discuss – talk or write about different sides of a topic.

Compare – show how different things are similar.

Contrast – show what makes things different.

Be sure to keep a running list in your notebook of all types of vocabulary words and their definitions. Always ask for the definition of a word you do not understand or look up the definition in a dictionary. Even after you look up a word, it is a good idea to ask your teacher to explain how the word relates to a specific subject. Teachers know that vocabulary is a major stumbling block for many students and are happy to assist you.

A PATH TO LEARNING AND LITERACY

STUDY CHARTS

Study Charts are key organizational tools. Learning and studying are two reasons for developing and using Study Charts.

Charts are a way to gather information. Study charts have headings and columns. The headings offer a methodical system for organizing information into categories. The columns offer lists of items in a similar category. When you are learning information, it is helpful to work with a chart. The chart may or may not supply partial information; your task is to complete the chart by adding the missing information. When the chart is completed you have a valuable and concise overview of a body of related information.

Charts can be used to review information. When you are studying, you can organize the material you are studying into charts. The following is an example.

Math formulas	Area	Perimeter	Description
Square	SxS=A	4S or S+S+S+S=P	4 equal sides
Rectangle	LxW=A	2L+2W=P	4 sided figure with opposite sides parallel
Circle	TTrxr=A	TTd=C	Round

A PATH TO LEARNING AND LITERACY

VISUAL WEBS

Visual webs are used to see information. There are many terms that fall into the category of Visual Webs. The use of visuals is an important key to enhanced learning. When you use a Visual Web, you see relationships.

CONCEPT MAPS – will give a full picture of a topic or unit of study. The main idea will be the focal point of the Concept Map and the Supporting Details will be linked to the main idea. The level of detail will vary depending on the message. When you construct a Concept Web you demonstrate your understanding of how a unit is connected.

A PATH TO LEARNING AND LITERACY

DIAGRAMS – offer a method to explain a topic by illustrating it. They could show Cause and Effect, Sequencing, Order of Operations, etc. This visual learning tool is an excellent study technique to build your personal understanding of a topic.

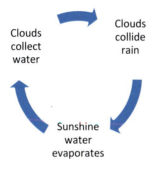

TIMELINES – are a tool for measurement. They illustrate Cause and Effect and Sequencing. Timelines build understanding by illustrating a bigger picture of a topic. In History, a timeline shows a series of events and what they can lead to. They can show advancement and progress. They can be used to extract inferences and understanding. Use a timeline when studying to help you make inferences and explain your understanding of items found on the timeline. Constructing a timeline can show

A PATH TO LEARNING AND LITERACY

Cause and Effect or the development of a broader topic.

Title: Major Events of World War II

Pearl Harbor	Midway	Coral Sea	D-Day	Hiroshima
1941	1942	1943	1944	1945

VENN DIAGRAMS – are used to illustrate similarities and differences. Similarities will be found in the overlapping portions of the circles and differences will be found in the separate portions of the circles. Remember compare means to show similarities and contract means to show differences.

Comparing and Contrasting Two Literary Works

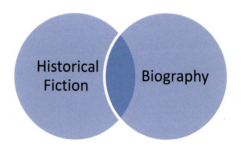

A PATH TO LEARNING AND LITERACY

SUMMARIES

Summaries are mini versions of what you learned. Summarizing is a process for explaining information in your own words. If you want to maximize each day's learning, you should write a few sentences explaining your classroom experience for that day. This is called keeping a process journal and it provides an immediate reinforcement of learning while building your retention and comprehension.

At the conclusion of a unit of study when you want to prepare for written exams, you need to explain the content using your own words. A method for writing summaries is as follows:

- Knowledge – Make a list of the key words for the unit you are studying.
- Organize – Place the words in order or a sequence that shows the development of information and/or ideas.
- Develop – Identify a logical way to explain your content.
- Write – Put your thoughts into words about the topic using specific information and examples.

A PATH TO LEARNING AND LITERACY

Using these skills reinforces your understanding of the content and teaches you self-confidence in your ability to express your ideas in written form.

When writing, be sure to follow the standard essay format – introduction, body, and conclusion. Your opening paragraph should introduce your topic. The body could be a few paragraphs that develop your topic and supply examples. The concluding paragraph pulls your ideas together.

A PATH TO LEARNING AND LITERACY

VERBALIZING

Verbalizing means saying aloud or talking about the information you need to master. Oral summaries are effective in reviewing information. When you verbalize a topic, you are forced to think about what you will say. It is called Thinking on Your Feet. When doing this, it is helpful to work with a list of related items/terms that you must include in your oral summary.

Oral summaries test your understanding of vocabulary and content. They develop organization skills and give you a chance to make connections in content.

Consider combining Oral Summaries with Webbing. Use the visual web to demonstrate relationships while you explain the various items included in the web. You will be amazed at the clarity of content that will result.

Oral Summaries are an excellent way to study with others. Research has proven that the most effective way to learn something is to teach it to others. Studying together accomplishes this strategy. Studying with another person is an

A PATH TO LEARNING AND LITERACY

opportunity to get and give immediate feedback and assure accuracy. The discussion of the topic can possibly expand to include new ideas and insights.

A PATH TO LEARNING AND LITERACY

A PATH TO LEARNING AND LITERACY

The Workbook

Learn how to study successfully by understanding and applying the study principles discussed in...

A Path to Learning and Literacy
Study Guide and Workbook for
Secondary Students and Parents

The contents of *The Workbook* supplement the information contained in **A PATH TO LEARNING AND LITERACY**. The fill-in pages for each chapter assist you in applying the information contained in the corresponding chapters in the book. Completing them will help you identify and understand your personal study habits. The worksheets in **Self-Assessment and Achievement**, relate to ideas discussed in the book for monitoring and recording personal progress, analyzing feedback, and developing your own path to learning.

A PATH TO LEARNING AND LITERACY

Workbook
Table of Contents

Section 1   Getting Started   p. 137
            Chapters 1-3

Section 2   Progress   p. 147
            Chapters 4-6

Section 3   Accomplishment   p. 159
            Chapters 7-9

Section 4   Self-Assessment   p. 169
            and Achievement

A PATH TO LEARNING AND LITERACY

SECTION 1
Getting Started

A PATH TO LEARNING AND LITERACY

A PATH TO LEARNING AND LITERACY
Chapter 1 Location, Time, and Materials...

Worksheet – Where, when, and with what will you work and study?

When planning your studying routine, it is important to specifically define what you will be doing. There are two things to consider – the first is where and when you will study, and the second is what materials you will need to study without disruption.

Step 1 – Where and when will you study?

    A. Where will you study?

    B. Why is this the best place for you to study?

    C. If you cannot study there, where is the next best place to study?

    D. Which subjects require homework?

    E. How much time do you need to complete your homework assignments?

A PATH TO LEARNING AND LITERACY

F. When is the best time for you to begin studying every day?

G. Is there anything that could disrupt this specific study time?

H. What will you do if you cannot begin studying at this time?

Step 2 - What materials will you need to do your studying?

    A. Which supplies will you need?

    B. What textbooks or other materials do you need?

    C. If you are using a computer, do you need website addresses? What are they?

Step 3 – Fill in the summary form below.

1. WHERE AND WHEN WILL YOU BE STUDYING?	2. WHAT DO YOU NEED TO STUDY?
Location	Supplies
Alternate location	Textbooks
Amount of time	Other materials
Start Time Finish Time	Computer – yes/no Website

A PATH TO LEARNING AND LITERACY

A PATH TO LEARNING AND LITERACY
Chapter 2 Identifying the Task

Worksheet – What do you have to do?

When sitting down to do your homework, it is important for you to know what you are expected to do. By answering the following questions, it will help focus your homework time.

Step 1 – Verbalize the task

    A.   What is the assignment?

    B.   Can you restate the assignment in your own words?

Step 2 – Know the assignment specifics.

    A.   When is your assignment due?

    B.   What books and materials do you need to do the assignment?

    C.   Do you have everything you need to do the assignment?

A PATH TO LEARNING AND LITERACY

D. For reading assignments, do you have the necessary books?

E. For writing assignments, do you know the correct format?

F. What is the correct format?

G. For worksheets, do you know the sections to be completed?

Step 3 – Are you working with another classmate?

A. If working with someone else, do you know their email or phone number?

B. Do you know what each person is responsible for doing?

A PATH TO LEARNING AND LITERACY

Step 4 – How will your homework or project be evaluated or graded?

    A.   *Are you using a rubric?*

    B.   *Did you meet all the criteria?*

    C.   *Did you review any previous feedback from your teacher for ways to improve your work?*

A PATH TO LEARNING AND LITERACY

A PATH TO LEARNING AND LITERACY
Chapter 3 Process

Worksheet – What is your plan to accomplish the task?

It is important to have a feeling of satisfaction and accomplishment when you are doing homework. You get that when you work efficiently and effectively. By answering the following questions, it will help you establish a workable plan for completing assignments.

Step 1 – Start with the end in mind and visualize what your assignment should look like.

    A. Do you know what is expected or do you still have some questions? If you have questions, be sure to ask your teacher.

    B. Is a Heading or Cover Page required?

    C. What are the details of the assignment?

    D. Do you have to write your answers in full sentences or are you completing a worksheet?

A PATH TO LEARNING AND LITERACY

    E.   Will you be using the computer? If so, which programs and/or websites?

Step 2 – Is reading part of the assignment?

    A.   Have you taken the time to **Preview** the reading portion of the assignment?
(See Section 4 Self-Assessment and Achievement)

    B.   Have you reviewed any questions at the end of the reading selection?

    C.   Have you read the assignment carefully?

Step 3 – How much time will you need to complete the assignment?

    A.   Is the assignment a daily assignment **OR** a long term assignment?

A PATH TO LEARNING AND LITERACY

B. If this is a long-term assignment
    1. What is the due date?

    2. How many days do you have to complete the assignment?

    3. How much time each day should you devote to completing the assignment?

C. Do you need to record and plan your time on a weekly/monthly calendar?

D. Did you add 10% more time to allow for ample time to complete the assignment?

A PATH TO LEARNING AND LITERACY

SECTION 2

Progress

A PATH TO LEARNING AND LITERACY

A PATH TO LEARNING AND LITERACY
Chapter 4 Listening

Worksheet – What information is being communicated?

Listening is an essential skill. It involved hearing what others say and understanding their message. Listening also involves paying attention to written feedback you receive from your teachers. The following steps will help you build stronger listening skills.

Step 1 – What do you do when you are listening?

    A. Do you give the person who is speaking your full attention?

    B. Can you relate to what others are saying?

    C. Do you value the information you are hearing?

    D. Do you observe the body language and gestures of the person talking?

    E. Do you react to what you hear?

A PATH TO LEARNING AND LITERACY

Step 2 – It is important to listen to content and instructions.

    A. Do you understand the topic your teacher is talking about?

    B. Do you know what follow-up activities are required?

    C. Did you receive instructions on what to do?

    D. Do you understand the directions you received?

    E. Can you express the content and/or instructions in your own words?

Step 3 – When you receive comments (feedback) about your work from others do you listen to their thoughts?

    A. Do you use the comments to evaluate your work?

    B. How do you react when you receive a grade?

C. When your teacher writes comments on your work do you read them and look for ways to improve your work?

D. Do you ever ask your teacher to explain his/her comments?

Step 4 – What can you do to improve your performance based on the information you receive about your work?

A. Have you learned some ways to improve your work?

B. Do you need to improve the way you write down your assignments?

C. Do you need to read test questions and directions more carefully?

A PATH TO LEARNING AND LITERACY

Step 5 – Can you practice active listening skills?

    A.   Can you accurately repeat what others say?

    B.   Can you follow a discussion and understand the details?

    C.   Is it easier to study with another person when you listen to each other?

    D.   In classroom situations do you need to take notes while listening?

A PATH TO LEARNING AND LITERACY

A PATH TO LEARNING AND LITERACY
Chapter 5 Learning

Worksheet – How do you acquire new information?

Everyone learns in different ways; it is called multimodal learning. You decide which method is the best way for you to learn. If you learn by hearing you are an auditory learner. If you need to see what you learn, you are a visual learner, and if you like to touch things when you learn you are a tactile learner. The truth is we all use all these learning styles to some deqree.

Step 1 – How do you review the new information you acquire in class?

    A. Do you take notes while listening in class?

    B. Do you read and recite your daily notes?

    C. Do you identify new vocabulary words related to content?

    D. Do you understand what information is being asked in all questions?

A PATH TO LEARNING AND LITERACY

Step 2 – What tools have you used to acquire new information?

    A.   Do you know how to preview your textbook? (See Section 4 - Self-Assessment and Achievement)

    B.   Are you familiar with the computer programs you need to use?

    C.   Do you have a list of the websites needed to do your work?

    D.   Can you successfully read your notes after taking them?

    E.   Do you use your notebook to study and is it organized?

    F.   Do you use an agenda book or assignment pad?

A PATH TO LEARNING AND LITERACY

Step 3 – What types of notes do you take?

    A.   Do you always record the date before taking notes?

    B.   Can you read your notes after you have taken them?

    C.   Do you read your notes to review content and fill in any additional information within 24 hours?

    D.   Do you highlight or underline key terms in your notes?

    E.   Do you use diagrams or other illustrations to enhance your notes?

A PATH TO LEARNING AND LITERACY

Step 4 – Do you use notes to help you plan your writing?

    A. Have you made a list of all facts you want to include in your writing?

    B. Can you organize your list of facts in the order in which you want to write about them?

    C. When writing, do you give examples to support your ideas?

    D. When writing, do you develop your ideas in a logical order?

Step 5 – Do you reread and edit your written work for content, style, and grammar?

A PATH TO LEARNING AND LITERACY

A PATH TO LEARNING AND LITERACY
Chapter 6 Studying

Worksheet – How do you go about studying?

Studying is a learned skill that you develop over time. It involves applying certain methods for retaining information. While you may be a visual, auditory or "hands on" learner it is important to remember to employ a portion of all these skills when studying. Also, it is important to use all sources of information when studying.

Step 1 – What materials should you assemble when getting ready to study?

    A. Identify the pages in your notebook that you should include in your studying.

    B. Which homework assignments did you complete during this unit of study?

    C. Did you receive any hand-out materials you are responsible for knowing?

    D. Which pages in your textbook are related to the unit of study?

    E. Are there any vocabulary words that you must know the meaning of?

A PATH TO LEARNING AND LITERACY

    F.   Is there any information from websites that you are responsible for including in the unit of study?

Step 2 – What type of test will you be taking?

    A.   Are there short answer questions?

    B.   Are there multiple-choice questions?

    C.   Will you have to write short response answers?

    D.   Will you be required to write extended responses?

Step 3 – Now that you know what to study and the type of test to study for, how will you study? *(See Section 4 – Self-Assessment and Achievement)*

    A.   Have you drilled yourself on vocabulary, formulas, or information you must commit to memory?

    B.   Did you make up any memory devises or flash cards to help you remember key information or a series of facts?

    C.   Did you read all notes and related information aloud several times?

A PATH TO LEARNING AND LITERACY

D. Can you verbally summarize what you have been studying?

E. Can you teach the information you are studying to someone else?

F. Have you practiced answering questions like the ones you will see on the test?

G. Are you prepared to analyze graphics?

H. Did you use Venn diagrams, curriculum webs, timelines, or other visuals to help you study?

I. Did you prepare for extended responses by writing paragraphs?

J. Did you make a list of key terms and information to include in your extended response?

A PATH TO LEARNING AND LITERACY

SECTION 3
Accomplishment

A PATH TO LEARNING AND LITERACY

A PATH TO LEARNING AND LITERACY
Chapter 7 Evaluation

Worksheet – How is your academic performance?

Evaluation is part of learning. Learning and studying are the skills you need in school. Evaluation is the feedback that tells you if you are learning all the information required and if your studying techniques are giving you the ability to express your knowledge. It is extremely important to give careful attention to evaluation. Evaluation is the key to continually improve your performance.

Step 1 – How did you do on your tests, homework, or projects?

    A.   What was your best grade?

    B.   What did you do to receive that grade?

    C.   When did you make the greatest improvement in your work?

    D.   Which learning and study habits are you most comfortable with?

    E.   What was your poorest score?

    F.   Which type(s) of questions did you find the most difficult?

A PATH TO LEARNING AND LITERACY

    G. How did you evaluate the results your received?

    H. Did you find the correct answers for the questions you got wrong?

Step 2 – How would you rate the quality of your work habits on a scale of 1 to 4?
(4 is the Best)

    A. Study Routine

    B. Understanding Assignments

    C. Completing Assignments

    D. Understanding Class Work

    E. Studying for Tests

    F. Reviewing Test Results

    G. Making needed changes when indicated.

Step 3 – How can you examine the mistakes you made? *(See Section 4 – Self-Assessment and Achievement)*

    A. Are you having trouble with reading and vocabulary?

    B. Did you analyze your test results and compare them to previous tests?

A PATH TO LEARNING AND LITERACY

    C.   Knowing what you now know is there something you would do differently when studying?

    D.   What can you do to improve your performance?

Step 4 – What steps will you take to continually improve your work?

    A.   What is your plan?

    B.   Did you verbalize this plan to yourself?

    C.   Did you share this plan with someone else?

A PATH TO LEARNING AND LITERACY

A PATH TO LEARNING AND LITERACY
Chapter 8 Achievement

Worksheet – What have you accomplished?

Each day we accomplish something. Sometimes we feel we fall short of meeting our goals and we can be too hard on ourselves. That is when it is important to remain positive and complete the **Inventory of Successes** *(See Section 4 – Self-Assessment and Achievement). Remember success is measured by the steps you take toward achieving your goal not only by the results. Sometimes it is necessary to take a different path or add new steps to your current path. Always be proud of yourself and your hard work.*

Step 1 – Do you have a good understanding of what your responsibilities are in school?

    A.   Are your assignments completed on time?

    B.   Is the information you study accurate?

    C.   Are you asking questions when you do not understand a topic or directions?

    D.   Have you reviewed your test results?

Step 2 – What accomplishment are you most proud of?

    A.   Why are you proud of this accomplishment?

    B.   What did you learn while working on this item/topic?

A PATH TO LEARNING AND LITERACY

    C.   How can you transfer that learning to other items/topics?

Step 3 – Did you take responsibility for your report card grades?

    A.   Are you satisfied with the grades you received?

    B.   Which grade are you most proud of?

    C.   Which grade do you think you could improve?

    D.   Can you name two things you would like to do differently after reviewing your report card?

Step 4 – Do you share your accomplishments and disappointments?

    A.   Who are you most comfortable sharing this information with?

    B.   Do you listen to comments/feedback?

    C.   Do you take the time to praise yourself when you feel satisfied?

A PATH TO LEARNING AND LITERACY

A PATH TO LEARNING AND LITERACY
Chapter 9 Celebration

Worksheet – Are you ready to celebrate?

*Celebrating is always fun, but it is more fun when you know you have earned it. Making strides in your schoolwork after establishing and following routines is a great feeling. Review your **Inventory of Successes** and take the time to be proud of your accomplishments. You know what you like and more importantly you know what you have earned. So, plan your celebrations accordingly. However, complete the process by compiling your **Things I Still Need or Want To Do** list (See Section 4 Self-Assessment and Achievement) and identify the things you still want to learn or the skills you have to continue working on.*

Step 1 – What have you learned about your ability to do schoolwork?

    A. What was your greatest accomplishment?

    B. Which area did you have to work hardest at in order to make improvements?

    C. What accomplishment are you most proud of?

    D. Which area would you like to improve next?

Step 2 – Did you receive any recognitions from your class, your teacher, or your school?

    A. Has any of your work been displayed?

    B. Have you received any certificates of achievement?

    C. Have you participated in any competitions?

    D. What kinds of changes have you seen on your report card?

A PATH TO LEARNING AND LITERACY

Step 3 – What are some of the best things you have done in school?

      A. Why did you enjoy them?

      B. What did you learn from them?

      C. Is there anything else you would like to do?

      D. Are you continually setting new goals?

Step 4 – Are you planning to celebrate your achievements?

      A. Who do you want to celebrate with?

      B. How and where will you celebrate?

      C. Do you appreciate the recognition you receive when you celebrate?

Congratulations!

Remember: Success takes Discipline, Discovery and Determination.

A PATH TO LEARNING AND LITERACY

SECTION 4
Self-Assessment and Achievement

Academic Performance Survey	p. 170
Previewing for Improved Reading Comprehension	p. 172
Taking Notes & Planning to Write	p. 174
Test Preparation Guide	p. 177
Homework/Test/Report Feedback Review	p. 179
Academic Progress Chart	p. 180
Inventory of Success	p. 181
My Most Memorable List	p. 182
Things I Still Need or Want to Learn	p. 183

A PATH TO LEARNING AND LITERACY
ACADEMIC PERFORMANCE SURVEY

Survey Question	Always (4)	Frequently (3)	Sometimes (2)	Never (1)
Do You do your daily homework in the same location?				
Do you understand what is expected in an assignment?				
Can you explain the content of a lesson in your own words?				
Do you preview reading materials in a textbook or online				
When studying for test do you know what to study?				
Are you familiar with the types of questions on the test?				
Do you review all results and feedback to see how you can improve?				

A PATH TO LEARNING AND LITERACY

Where are you on the PATH TO SUCCESS?

TOTAL SCORE: _____

EVALUATION:

    24-28 Work and study habits have you on a path to success.

    21-25 Work and study habits show outstanding discovery and determination.

    14-20 Work and study habits reflect some discipline and determination

    7-13 Work and study habits need discipline, and determination.

A PATH TO LEARNING AND LITERACY

A PATH TO LEARNING AND LITERACY
Previewing for Improved Reading Comprehension

Reading is the key to all learning. **Previewing** is a process for anticipating what you will read. When reading a textbook, it is important to follow the steps listed below for **Previewing**. Initially, it takes effort to learn how to preview, but once you are familiar with the process, it will be fast and easy and increase your reading comprehension and speed. Here is a guide for **Previewing** what you read.

Subject: _____

Assignment_____

A. Identify and read the title of the chapter section or selection you will be reading.

B. Locate and read all bold face headings (topics) in the selection. These are the key facts to help focus your reading.

C. Notice any words in **bold** or *italics* and be sure you understand the meaning of each of those words. Use the textbook's glossary to find the meaning.

D. Locate all graphics and pictures in the reading selection. Read the caption for each item for an explanation of the visual.

A PATH TO LEARNING AND LITERACY

E. Check to see if there are questions at the conclusion of the reading selection. Read them because they will focus your reading.

F. Using the above information to verbalize what you will be reading about.

Now you are ready to read your assignment.

A PATH TO LEARNING AND LITERACY

A PATH TO LEARNING AND LITERACY
Taking Notes and Planning to Write

You take notes to help you remember key information. When listening to lectures or stories you will want to take notes to highlight the topical information. During class you may take notes to review and study the information. Taking notes is a learned skill. You should also use notes to plan and organize writing assignments or research projects.

TAKING NOTES

A. **Fill-In Notes** are used to find key words or ideas in an assignment. Completing a sentence or doing workbook activities are examples of Fill-In Notes.

B. **Bullet Notes** are an easy and successful method for taking notes while listening. Each time you hear a key factor or term you make a bullet and record your fact in one or two words.

C. **Given Notes** are notes you copy from a whiteboard, chalkboard or overhead. You can also be given a handout with notes. When receiving these pre-prepared notes, it is important to make sure you read and understand them. Be sure to underline or highlight key words and terms.

D. Outline Notes organize your information according to main topics and supporting details. Outline notes are helpful when planning a written assignment such as an essay or research paper. Outline notes use numbers and letters to promote organization.

The model below uses **Outline Notes** to review and explain note taking.

For Example:
- I. All Notes are Helpful
  - A. Fill-in Notes
  - B. Bullet Notes
  - C. Given Notes
  - D. Outline Notes
- II. Writing Essays and Reports
  - A. Outline Notes
    1. Main Topic
    2. Supporting Details
  - B. Planning Notes
    1. Introduction
    2. Body of Report
    3. Summary
  - C. Commentary and Reaction Notes
    1. Conclusion
    2. Opinion
    3. Inference

A PATH TO LEARNING AND LITERACY

Planning Notes *are used when you review the notes you have taken and decide how to use them. If you are writing an essay you will decide which notes to use in an introduction, and which to use in the body of the writing and how these ideas support your conclusion.*

Commentary and Reaction Notes *help support decisions, conclusions, opinions, and help you make inferences. This is a higher order thinking skill and requires you to read and review information and see relationships such as cause and effect. You can give an opinion or reaction and support how you reached that opinion. You can predict what will happen next based on what you have presented in your writing.*

Here is a template to follow when writing an essay.

Title
Opening Paragraph
Topic sentence- Introduce what you are writing about.
Middle Paragraph(s)
Give(s) information and details related to the topic of the essay. Include examples to enhance information.
Final Paragraph
Summarizes what you have stated. Can draw conclusions or give opinions based on content.

A PATH TO LEARNING AND LITERACY

A PATH TO LEARNING AND LITERACY
Test Preparation Guide

Subject_____

Date of Test_____

Types of Questions_____

Review the diagram below to determine what sources contain information you should be studying for an upcoming test. Be sure to use all related materials when studying for a test.

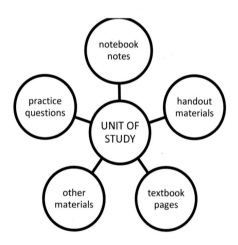

Now fill in the chart below with the specific **information you will study** *for an upcoming test.*

A PATH TO LEARNING AND LITERACY

Be sure to list what you have in other materials. For example, this could be math formulas, vocabulary lists, or graphs and charts.

What unit is your test on?
_____

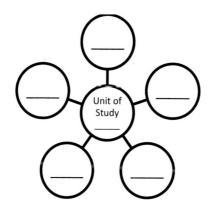

OTHER MATERIALS YOU NEED TO STUDY

-
-
-
-
-

A PATH TO LEARNING AND LITERACY

A PATH TO LEARNING AND LITERACY
Homework/Test/Report Feedback Review

Use this form to self- evaluate the grade you received.

Subject_____

Assignment_____

Grade/Score_____

Are you satisfied with the grade you received? Why?

Did you review your mistakes to determine why you missed certain questions?

What can you do to correct those mistakes?

Do you know how your teacher determined your grade?

Do you have questions about your grade?

If yes, what are those questions? Be sure to discuss them with your teacher.

What have you learned from this work that will help you to improve your performance?

A PATH TO LEARNING AND LITERACY

A PATH TO LEARNING AND LITERACY
Academic Progress Chart

As you learn many ways to improve your studying habits it is important to keep track of which strategies work for you, the progress you are making and the areas where your work is improving. Use this chart to keep a record of your progress. Be sure to record whether your grade is going up or down and the reason why. This will help you learn the best ways for you to study.

Subject	Date	Grade	Assign.	Feedback
SAMPLE Social Studies	10/13	91	test	Improved/better essay

A PATH TO LEARNING AND LITERACY

A PATH TO LEARNING AND LITERACY
Inventory of Success

When you apply yourself in studying and you use the methods for improvement that are described in the book you will appreciate your achievements. Rate your progress each week or each month to determine how you are doing. Write the date you are doing your Inventory of Successes on the top line under Date and rate yourself in each of the areas of measurement listed in the first column.

The rating scale is as follows: 4 = Outstanding Effort, 3= Good Effort, 2= Satisfactory Effort, 1= Needs Effort

Area of Measurement	Date	Date	Date	Date
Establishing and Following Routines				
Verbalizing Assignments				
Completing Homework as scheduled				
Reviewing Class Notes Regularly				
Listening and Following Instructions				
Planning & Studying for Tests				
Self-Assessing my Performance				

A PATH TO LEARNING AND LITERACY

A PATH TO LEARNING AND LITERACY
My Most Memorable List

Complete each of the following sentence beginnings with examples of your completed work.

My most enjoyable activity was

The assignment where I tried my hardest was

The assignment that gave me the most trouble was

I was most satisfied with

I think I learn best by

When I study, I need to

The person I like to share my feelings about school with is

When I ask my teacher a question, I expect

The questions on a test that give me the most trouble are

I know my grades will improve when I

I will never forget doing

A PATH TO LEARNING AND LITERACY

A PATH TO LEARNING AND LIERACY
Things I Still Need or Want to Learn

The more you learn the more you will want to learn. Making lists helps you focus your attention and effort in setting and accomplishing personal goals.

    A. **List five things** you still need to do to improve your learning and studying routines.

For example, you may need to learn to write complete paragraphs.

    1.
    2.
    3.
    4.
    5.

Short term goal: Choose one of the items above and write a sentence about what you should do to reach that goal.

    B. **List five things** you would like to learn more information about.

For example, you might want to find out about space travel.

    1.
    2.
    3.
    4.
    5.

Long term goal: Choose one of the items above and discuss it with an adult. Decide how you can get more information on the topic.

Keep Studying, Keep Learning, Keep succeeding!

A PATH TO LEARNING AND LITERACY

A PATH TO LEARNING AND LITERACY

ABOUT THE AUTHOR

Claire Johnson Machosky-Ullman holds a Bachelor of Arts in History and Government from Adelphi University and a Master of Science in School Administration from Long Island University. In 2012 she received **The Distinguished Alumni Award** from Adelphi University recognizing her accomplishments and dedication to her work in Education. Claire's career began with teaching 6th graders at Our Lady of Mercy Parochial School in Hicksville, N.Y. In 1963 she moved to the Hewlett-Woodmere Public Schools where Claire was a Social Studies classroom teacher in the middle school; to recognize her commitment to her classes, students nominated her for inclusion in **Who's Who Among America's Teachers.** Claire became the Social Studies Department Chairperson and School Dean before retiring in 2001.

During her tenure she brought "National History Day" to the school, beginning the school's long and accomplished success with the program. Her concern for all children inspired Claire to design and supervise the Middle School's Talented and Gifted Program, while assisting the Special Education Department with individualized curriculum instruction. To support her students, Claire became actively involved with the New York State Education Department. She became a question-writer for State Assessments, trained teachers in evaluation and grading, and gave workshops at Teacher Centers throughout Long Island. Claire became an Educational Consultant with Long Island BOCES (Board of Cooperative Education Services) upon her retirement from the classroom.

Claire Machosky is the co-editor of the New York State Social Studies Elementary Core Curriculum. Her career in writing began in 2002 and 2003 with two published articles on Middle School emphasizing that middle school is "All About the Children". The articles appeared in the New York State School Supervisors and Administrators Journal. In 2010 the first edition of **A Path to Learning and Literacy** was

A PATH TO LEARNING AND LITERACY

published followed in 2013 with **Study*Learn*Succeed**, a study book for children in the Primary Grades.

A dedicated educator, Claire guided students from around the world in the "Presidential Classroom" program in Washington, D.C.; received scholarships to attend programs on Canadian Studies at St. Lawrence University, and The Taft Seminar on Government at City College of New York. In 2006 she received a Phi Delta Kappa Scholarship to become a Visiting Scholar in PDKs travel program to London.

In 2013-14 Claire coordinated the Library of Congress's **Teaching with Primary Sources (TPS)** Grant for Eastern Suffolk BOCES on Long Island. She continues to be affiliated with the Library of Congress TPS Program out of Waynesburg University. Claire has shared her work at various professional conferences locally and nationally.

Claire is an educator, but most importantly a parent, and a grandparent. She is the mother of three grown children, and the grandmother of five. As a parent she was actively involved in her children's schools. Through her efforts Long Island's Wantagh School District implemented a Summer Recreation Program that served its children for over a quarter of a century. Claire was awarded **Honorary Lifetime Membership** in the National PTA in recognition for her dedication to the children of the community. Between 2010 and 2016 she coordinated the award-winning **Odyssey of the Mind** competition for her grandchildren's school in Virginia.

Claire and her husband, Al Ullman, are enjoying their active retirement in Northern Virginia. Claire co-chairs the Education Committee at the Hylton Performing Arts Center on the George Mason University Campus in Manassas, Virginia.

A PATH TO LEARNING AND LITERACY

ACKNOWLEDGEMENTS

The content of this book and the accompanying worksheets are my original works. During my career in education I attended post-graduate courses, workshops, lectures, and conferences giving me access to educational research and theory that became an integral part of my classroom instruction and my staff development seminars. I would like to recognize the following Leaders for their valuable contributions to Education; studying and learning their theories made me a better teacher.

Claire Johnson Machosky

Dr. Paul Black – Feedback, Formative Assessment
Dr. Alan Bloom – Higher Order Theory,
Bloom's Taxonomy
Dr. Steven R. Covey – *The 7 Habits of Highly Effective People*
Drs. Rita & Ken Dunn – Learning Styles
Dr. William Glasser – Research on Quality Schools
Dr. Madeline Hunter – Direct Instruction Model
Dr. Heidi Hayes Jacobs – Interdisciplinary Instruction
Drs. David W. Johnson & Roger T. Johnson
Cooperative Learning
Dr. Abraham Maslow – Hierarchy of Needs
Dr. Diane Ravitch – Educational Historian
Dr. Carol Tomlinson – Differentiated Instruction
Dr. Harry Wong – *The First Days of School*

A PATH TO LEARNING AND LITERACY

> *"SUCCESS TAKES DISCIPLINE, DISCOVERY AND DETERMINATION."*

September 2020